ROYAL BOROUGH

Follow us on twitter

Please return by the last date shown

Thank you! To renew, please contact any
Royal Greenwich library or renew online or by phone
www.better.org.uk/greenwichlibraries
24hr renewal line 01527 852384

The Thames
A Very Peculiar History™

With added tributaries

'Sweet Thames, run softly,
till I end my song.'

Edmund Spenser (1552–1599), Prothalamion

For William and Harriett,
whose friendship runs deep

DA

Editor: Nick Pierce

Artist: David Lyttleton
Additional artwork: Shutterstock

Published in Great Britain in MMXVIII by
Book House, an imprint of
The Salariya Book Company Ltd
25 Marlborough Place, Brighton BN1 1UB
www.salariya.com

ISBN: 978-1-912233-38-0

Visit
www.salariya.com
for our online catalogue and
free fun stuff.

The Thames

A Very Peculiar History™

With added tributaries

Written by
David Arscott

Created and designed by
David Salariya

BOOK HOUSE
a SALARIYA imprint

'You can't walk by the river at Cliveden
Reach and not believe in God.'
Stanley Spencer, artist

Glide gently, thus for ever glide,
O Thames! that other bards may see
As lovely visions by thy side
As now, fair river! come to me.
William Wordsworth: 'Remembrance of Collins'

And at my feet the pale green Thames
Lies like a rod of rippled jade.
Oscar Wilde: 'Symphony in Yellow'

'There is no river in the world to be
compared for majesty and the witchery
of association to the Thames.'
Hugh Nisbet, 'The Phantom Model'

'You absorb 2,000 years of history
just by being near the Thames.'
Martin Freeman, Sherlock Holmes actor

Contents

'...the silver thread
which runs through
the history
of Britain. '

LIQUID
HISTORY

O n board the Royal Yacht as it sailed up the Thames in May 1954, Sir Winston Churchill waxed lyrical to the young Queen Elizabeth.

'One saw this dirty commercial river as one came up', she recalled in a television interview more than thirty years later, 'and he was describing it as the silver thread which runs through the history of Britain.'

An earlier MP, John Elliot Burns, expressed that thought more succinctly. 'The Thames', he declared, 'is liquid history.'

If the Thames today is both cleaner and less busy with trade than half a century ago, Her Majesty's observation still has some traction: in certain moods and in certain stretches the river can appear sullen, uninviting and, in its swirls and eddies, sometimes plain dangerous.

But Churchill and Burns spoke the truth. It's impossible to strike up a close acquaintance with the Thames without becoming aware of the countless people who have colonised its foreshore and been carried on its tides, or of great events in the national and colonial story that have been played out on and around it.

The Museum of London displays some 90,000 objects recovered from its bed and surrounding silt – weapons, ornaments, coins, and a host of other things either lost or simply thrown away. Together they shape a narrative of relentless immigration and occupation; of the increasing importance of the river as a highway; of hamlets expanding into significant towns along its banks, drawing on its waters not only for transport but for their industrial and commercial uses – among them milling, fishing and farming on the fertile soils that run alongside.

The greatest of these, of course, is London itself. Without the river it would surely never have existed.

The power of ice

The river has its own history. Geologists tell us that in the distant past, when Britain was still attached to the Continent by a land bridge, the Thames flowed in a northerly direction to join what we now know as the Rhine.

Workmen digging out the railway line from Romford to Upminster in the 1890s discovered the dried-up bed of that earlier course. The Thames had then rolled through a tropical world of palm trees, turtles, lemurs, rhinos and crocodiles before the climate began to cool – culminating in a series of ice ages which saw advancing glaciers push the river southwards.

The warming that marked the end of the last ice age some ten thousand years ago unleashed the pent-up fury of overpowering melt waters. They burst through the chalk barrier of the Chilterns to create the Goring Gap through which the Thames now runs.

Small Beginnings

Where does the Thames rise? Officially, in a Gloucestershire meadow called Trewsbury Mead, otherwise known as Thames Head, near the village of Kemble. Here a stone bears the inscription: 'The Conservators of the river Thames 1857–1974. This stone was placed here to mark the source of the River Thames.'

In dry weather there's no sign of water at all, a fact which no doubt encourages those who prefer an alternative candidate for the source. This is at Seven Springs, to the north of Cirencester, where a plaque makes its claim in Latin – perhaps in an attempt to give it more authority. It reads: 'Hic Tuus O Tamesine Pater Septemgeminus Fons', or (to put it in English) 'Here, O Father Thames, is your seven-sourced fountain.'

This, to most neutrals, is the source of the River Churn (Celtic for 'swift'), which joins the Thames as a tributary at Cricklade. The argument may be academic, but note that if you choose to join the rebel camp you need to add a further 19 km (12 miles) to the river's official length.

It was a fast-flowing river then, alongside which new settlers hunted reindeer and elk with flint weapons and bows and arrows. 'It was the age in which', the novelist-cum-historian Peter Ackroyd has written with anachronistic fancy, 'hippos wallowed in Trafalgar Square and elephants roamed down the Strand.'

Here to stay

Once the Thames had settled to much the same course and size as it is today, and in a climate similar to our own, newcomers arrived in ever-increasing numbers.

- Close to the present-day Vauxhall Bridge the oak stumps of a Bronze Age bridge have been discovered, dated to about 1500 BC. Swords, rapiers and spears from roughly the same period may have been deposited in hoards as a kind of propitiation to the gods.

- Abingdon claims to be the oldest continually inhabited town in England, because its centre lies above the remains of a settlement in the Iron Age (from 800 BC).

- The Romans couldn't resist staking out the territory, and Julius Caesar twice made summer forays into Britain, in 55 and 54 BC. His is the first written account we have of the river: 'The Thames can be forded only at one place and that with difficulty.'

That situation wouldn't last for very long, thanks to Caesar's successors. After the emperor Claudius invaded Britain in AD 43 the Romans were in charge for almost four hundred years, and they set about running their new territory with customary efficiency – connecting new towns and country villas with their renowned straight roads and, of course, taming the river.

Their greatest achievement, at least in hindsight, was the creation of London. They erected a wooden bridge close to where London Bridge now stands, put up a protective wall (a few sections survive in the City) and built wharfs to create a thriving port.

By AD 120 London had a population of around 45,000 – a figure which, after a later decline, it would not reach again until the 13th century.

Saxons and Danes

For the Saxons who swept into Britain as the Roman empire collapsed in the 5th century AD, the Thames was both a barrier and a dangerous highway. When the country was divided between different kingdoms the river was a frontier between Mercia to the north and Wessex in the south. But it was also a route by which Viking longboats raced inland to inflict cruel damage on a vulnerable people.

Old father Thames

Many rivers have their tutelary gods and goddesses, but nobody knows when Old Father Thames first emerged as the personification of the river. He's always depicted as a bit of a hippy character, naked and with long flowing locks and a beard.

A statue by the very first lock on the Thames at Lechlade shows him with a spade slung over his shoulder. Originally commissioned in 1854 to stand in the grounds of the Crystal Palace in Hyde Park, it was later moved to the source at Thames Head, where it was vandalised.

In 851 no fewer than 350 of them came up the river, burning London to the ground, and they remained a threat even after King Alfred's victory at the Battle of Edington in 878 which restricted them to the Danelaw in the north. (He reclaimed the town, rebuilt the old centre and renamed it Lundenburh.) Indeed, in 1016 the country would be ruled by a Danish king – Cnut, or as we would rather know him, Canute.

The Saxon period saw the creation of much of the England we know: our parish boundaries, the villages inside them, the names we call them by, a vast array of churches and monasteries, the very language itself – and that legacy can be traced all along the Thames.

Setting the Thames on fire

It's a strange expression, usually used in the negative to suggest that someone isn't strong on wit or dynamism. One of Jane Austen's characters employs it like that in *Persuasion*, referring to Sir Walter Elliott:

'The Baronet will never set the Thames on fire, but there seems to be no harm in him.'

Oxford. The clue is in the name. The river was easily crossed here, and the town grew as a trading centre between Mercia and Wessex.

Kingston upon Thames. Ditto. This was the first royal borough in the country. Egbert held a great council here in 838, and several 10th-century kings were crowned at the 'coronation stone' now on display at the Guildhall, among them Aethelstan and Aethelred the Unready.

Dorchester-on-Thames (not to be confused with the county town of Dorset) was a Roman settlement. It later became the de facto capital of Saxon Wessex, until it was eventually displaced by Winchester.

Cricklade. The Romans were here, too, and they built the first bridge, but the place was completely remodelled on becoming one of 30 fortified towns built by Alfred to defend Wessex against the Danes.

Wallingford. Another crossing point, this was an Anglo-Saxon burgh with a mint – and the conquering Normans built a great castle at the spot after the Conquest in 1066.

The Thames in numbers

182 m (600 feet) fall from the source to the sea. Most of its descent occurs within the first 19 km (12 miles)

246 km (215 miles) in length. The longest river in England, and the second in Britain after the Severn

214 bridges

307 km (191 miles) navigable length

296 km (184 miles) – the length of the Thames Path to the Thames Barrier. An extension to Tilbury expands the walk to 346 km (215 miles)

80 islands

45 locks

38 named tributaries

7 metres (23 feet): the average rise in each tide

17 tunnels

6 public ferries

5 canals running from it

3 toll bridges

1 ford and cable car crossing

Kings and queens

For those who like their history top-down, there are plenty of associations between the river and our monarchs down the ages.

Look out on the left bank* near Staines Bridge and you'll see the so-called London Stone which was erected there in 1285. This marks the western extent of the Corporation of London's authority over the Thames at what was then – before locks were introduced dowstream – the upper limit of the tidal river. It's also a reminder of the fecklessness of Richard I (Lionheart), who in 1197 had sold those rights to the Corporation because he needed the cash to finance his crusades.

There have, naturally, been some bloody scenes. The little bridge of 1200 at Radcot, a quiet spot some 48 km (thirty miles) downstream from the source, was the scene of a skirmish involving Henry Bolingbroke, later Henry IV.

* By tradition the left/right designation refers to the orientation of the banks as you look downstream towards the sea.

A later account tells us that in 1387 Henry here put to flight an 800-strong force supportive of Richard II, but that Thomas Molineux, in trying to escape, found himself trapped in the water by the bridge. He climbed out, pleading for mercy, whereupon a knight 'caught him by the helmet, plucked it off his head, and straightways drawing his dagger, stroke him into the brains and so dispatched him'.

For the Tudors the Thames was the setting for gaudy pageants, for grand funeral processions – and for transporting the unfortunate to the dreaded Tower of London.

Henry VIII loved an over-the-top display on the water to celebrate his weddings although, as we know, there weren't always happy endings. When Anne Boleyn paraded down the river for her coronation in 1533, she was dressed in cloth of gold, and the retinue of decorated barges following in her wake, flags fluttering and bands playing, was said to extend for over 6 km (four miles).

Three years later she was taken down the river to her beheading.

Elizabeth I, like her father, was born at Greenwich Palace, and it wasn't far from there, at Tilbury, that she made her famous speech to the troops before the arrival of the Spanish Armada in 1588: 'I know I have the body of a weak and feeble woman; but I have the heart and stomach of a king, and of a king of England too.'

On her death in 1603 her body was carried to the Palace of Whitehall, inspiring a verse by the contemporary historian William Camden:

> The Queen was brought by water to White-hall
> At every stroake the oars did let tears fall:
> More clung about the Barge, fish under water
> Wept out their eyes of pearl, and swam blind after.

The Stuarts were as keen as the Tudors on riverine dramatics. When Charles II married Catherine of Braganza in 1662 he was rowed down the Thames as part of a pageant grandly entitled 'Acqua Triumphalis'. The diarist John Evelyn called it 'the most magnificent Triumph that ever floted on the Thames, considering the innumerable boates & Vessels, dressd and adornd with all imaginable Pomp'.

After the Great Fire of London in 1666, the king decided that the capital's rebuilding should include 'a fair key or wharf on all the river side'. His plan to sweep away the old mishmash of sheds and warehouses to create a swanky modern quayside on the left bank was only partially achieved, but it certainly demonstrated his priorities.

Dutch outrage

The Dutch delivered the greatest of insults to the Thames-loving Charles II in June, 1667 when their warships came up the river to Gravesend and took a right turn up the River Medway to the naval dockyard at Chatham.

Although the two countries were engaged in the Second Anglo-Dutch War, much of the English fleet had been mothballed because of a lack of funds. The Dutch bombarded Chatham and Gillingham, burned several ships and even towed away the English flagship HMS *Royal Charles*.

This devastating attack, one of the worst experiences in British naval history, led to a swift end to the war – on Dutch terms.

The benefits, as well as the pleasure, of making a big splash weren't lost on George I, who in 1717 was being given a rough ride, both domestically and politically, by his son, the Prince of Wales.

What better uplift than a magnificent boating party on the Thames to music especially commissioned from his court musician? So it was that George was wafted on a rising tide from Whitehall to Chelsea, with his two mistresses beside him and a 50-strong orchestra in the barge behind playing Handel's *Water Music*. He enjoyed himself so much that he had the whole work performed three times. It was a splendid PR coup.

Hoi polloi

If royalty isn't your thing, rest assured that the river has witnessed its share of bottom-up events too.

- In 890 at Shifford, west of Oxford, King Alfred held the first recorded English parliament – by no means democracy, but an early step along the way.

- In 1215, in a water meadow at Runnymede near Windsor, King John was obliged to sign that great 'bill of rights', Magna Carta. It influenced the early colonists in America and the formation of their Constitution in 1787: memorials at the site include one to US President John F. Kennedy, who 'died by an assassin's hand 22 November 1963'.

Pilgrimage

Although the *Mayflower* with its 102 Puritan would-be settlers set sail from Plymouth for America in July 1620, the starting point for the journey was in fact the ship's home port of Rotherhithe on the Thames.

While still on board, the pilgrims wrote the 'Mayflower Compact', the first written agreement about the government they meant to set up on arrival.

The captain, Christopher Jones, brought his ship back up the river to Rotherhithe in May 1621. He was dead within the year and is buried in St Mary's churchyard, where there's a memorial to him and a plaque commemorating the *Mayflower*'s voyage.

- The Putney Debates in 1647 were arranged by officers and soldiers of Oliver Cromwell's Model Army after the Civil War to discuss the future constitution of the country. Colonel Thomas Rainsborough made the famous Leveller statement: 'I think that the poorest he that is in England hath a life to live as the greatest he.'

- A little further downstream, at Westminster, under the watchful eye of Big Ben, stands that ultimate expression of the democratic tendency, 'the mother of parliaments'.

Rolling along

And Old Father Thames, if he could speak, what would he say about all the restless episodes of turmoil and glory, hope and despair that have been played out around him while, age by age, he has stroked his luxurious beard and looked on?

Probably – in the words of the celebrated song by Raymond Wallace and Betsy O'Hogan – that, fancy free, he just 'keeps rolling along/ Down to the mighty sea'.

Some things haven't changed very much. Once a barrier between Saxon kingdoms, the Thames now borders nine English counties and divides Wiltshire from Gloucestershire; Oxfordshire from Berkshire; Surrey from Middlesex; and Kent from Essex.

It remains tidal, of course, but the point at which the waters stop in their tracks changed with the construction of Teddington Lock in 1812. Richard the Lionheart's stone has been superseded by a boundary marker of 1909 at Teddington. The non-tidal Thames above it is now the responsibility of the Environment Agency, while the salty downstream section (the Tideway) is controlled by the Port of London Authority.

Old Father Thames would also shrug at historical events which have only by accident occurred in his backyard. 'Concentrate on my waters!' he might chide us – and that's what we shall be doing in this book.

The river now supplies two-thirds of London's drinking water. That, as we shall discover, would have been unthinkable in years gone by.

It's rich in wildlife where once it was little more than a chemical sink, and it's given over to pleasure and business where it once knew the dirt and toil of trade and industry.

And what of all the various people who have earned a living from the river, whether honestly or otherwise, over the years? They will be part of our theme, too.

'Still she haunts me,
phantomwise,
Alice moving under skies
Never seen by
waking eyes.'

CHAPTER ONE

TALES OF THE RIVERBANK

'**N**ever in his life had he seen a river before. All was a-shake and a-shiver – glints and gleams and sparkles, rustle and swirl, chatter and bubble. The Mole was bewitched.'

Just as Kenneth Grahame himself was: the author of *The Wind in the Willows* spent a few magical childhood years in and around the village of Cookham on the banks of the upper Thames, later recreated that world of blissful memory in the stories he wrote for his son, and after his retirement returned to his beloved riverside some kilometres away at Pangbourne.

The tranquillity of the non-tidal Thames – and of the lonelier reaches near its source in particular – was an inspiration to a bevy of writers born in the Victorian era. These are the areas least changed today, which gives their work a timeless quality.

Here's Hilaire Belloc, whose *The Historic Thames* was published in the same year (1908) as Grahame's adventures of Mole, Ratty and Mr Toad: 'You might put a man of the fifteenth century on to the water below St. John's Lock, and until he came to Buscot Lock he would hardly know that he had passed into a time other than his own.'

The narrator of William Morris's utopian novel *News from Nowhere* travels along the river by boat and exults in 'the slender stream of the Thames winding below us between the garden of a country I have been telling of; a furlong from us was a beautiful little islet begrown with graceful trees; on the slopes westward of us was a wood of varied growth overhanging the narrow meadow on the south side of the river; while to the north was a wide stretch of mead rising very gradually from the river's edge.'

Morris was a late-comer to the Thames. The writer, textile designer and social activist was a townie until his late thirties, when he looked for a family retreat in the country and found a stone Elizabethan house to rent 3 km (two miles) above Radcot bridge at Kelmscott. (For some reason he preferred to call his place Kelmscott Manor with a double-t, just as his publishing house in London would be the Kelmscott Press.) He enjoyed a glimpse of the Thames from his south-facing window.

In 1880, by now in his mid-fifties, he made a grand procession up the river from his Hammersmith home to Kelmscott Manor.

Eyots

An eyot, pronounced (and sometimes spelt) 'ait', is one of the many small islands in the Thames.

A few are artificial, to separate locks from their weirs. Most, though, are natural – and you'll find them at their most plentiful around Oxford, where the river divides into several streams across the floodplain.

Morris was joined by his wife, his two daughters and some friends, and their adventure had its comical side. At the front, with a place for two rowers, was a houseboat called *The Ark*, hired from an Oxford boatyard and described by one of the party as 'a mechanical tin kettle' and by Morris's daughter May as 'a sort of insane gondola'. It towed in its wake a rowing boat named *Alfred*.

They took six days over the journey, Morris sleeping in the *Ark* overnight while everyone else put up at towns along the way – and they enjoyed it so much that they did it all over again the following year.

Curiouser and curiouser

Few river idylls can compare with our image of an Oxford Mathematics don gliding along the Thames in a rowing boat while enthralling his young companions with weird tales of a girl's adventures underground.

He, of course, was Charles Dodgson, a.k.a Lewis Carroll, and his wonderfully imaginative stories became *Alice in Wonderland*.

Alice Liddell, his favourite for whom the story was told, remembered the moment years later:

The beginning of Alice was told to me one summer afternoon, when the sun was so hot we landed in the meadows down the river, deserting the boat to take refuge in the only bit of shade to be found, which was under a newly made hayrick.

Another time the story would begin in the boat and Mr. Dodgson would pretend to fall asleep in the middle, to our great dismay.

Upper/Middle

Aficionados distinguish between the Upper Thames, from the source to Newbridge, and the Middle Thames, down to the tidal barrier at Teddington Lock.

This second stretch has many attractive features, but it's busier and meets a succession of towns along the way: Oxford, Reading, Henley-on-Thames, Marlow, Maidenhead, Windsor, Staines and Kingston-upon-Thames.

The Isis conundrum

Since our river was known as Tamesas to the Celts, appears in Latin as Tamesis, became Temese in Middle English, is given as Tamisiam in Magna Carta and is pronounced 'Tems', it's very odd to find it spelt Thames. Someone, perhaps in Renaissance times, stuck in that rogue 'h' (was it to give it a posh Greek feeling?), and everyone followed suit.

As for the origins of the name, let's not go there. Some experts have suggested that it means 'dark', but it's etymological guesswork.

Another mystery is that the stretch of the Thames on which Lewis Carroll rowed with Alice is known as the Isis. The name is commonly applied to the 3 kilometres or so (2 miles) between Iffley Lock and Osney Lock, although OS maps give the river that grand title all the way upriver to Dorchester.

Here's another piece of antiquarian nonsense: The River Thame joins the Thames near Dorchester, so some bright spark regarded 'Tamesis' as meaning a confluence of the Thame with the Isis. There's always a sucker for any daft theory.

Here's part of a poem Carroll wrote about those golden moments:

> A boat beneath a sunny sky,
> Lingering onward dreamily
> In an evening of July –
>
> Children three that nestle near,
> Eager eye and willing ear,
> Pleased a simple tale to hear –
>
> Long has paled that sunny sky:
> Echoes fade and memories die:
> Autumn frosts have slain July.
>
> Still she haunts me, phantomwise,
> Alice moving under skies
> Never seen by waking eyes.

Healing waters

The peace of an unspoiled river scene, together with the cleansing and nourishing qualities of water, no doubt explain the harnessing of the Thames for religious rites and for health cures – albeit, sad to say, that these have included some examples of no-good quackery.

St Augustine, the Benedictine monk who brought Christianity to England at the end of the sixth century, is said to have healed the blind in a miracle at Cricklade, where there was one of at least 26 healing springs that have been identified next to the Thames.

Baptisms were once commonplace in the river – a spot at Cricklade was being used for the purpose as late as the early 20th century, while a stone font near the bridge at Radcot was used for baptismal rites.

In 634 Bishop Birinius immersed King Cynegius of Wessex at Dorchester in the presence of Oswald, the Christian king of Northumbria, so uniting the two realms against the pagan kingdom of Mercia.

We even find the spiritual aspect of the river surfacing in *The Wind in the Willows*. As Rat accompanies Mole to a Thames eyot 'with solemn expectation' of finding the river deity, he whispers, 'This is the place of my song-dream, the place the music played to me. Here, in this holy place, here if anywhere, surely we shall find Him.'

A Cookham visionary

Few English painters have been stranger than Stanley Spencer, who believed Cookham (where he was born) to be 'a village in heaven', and who used local people in religious scenes he re-imagined as taking place there.

The most remarkable is *The Resurrection, Cookham*, which was greeted as a masterpiece when it was first unveiled in 1927, the art critic of *The Times* declaring 'It is as if a pre-Raphaelite had shaken hands with a cubist'. It depicts Spencer, his friends and his family emerging from their graves in Holy Trinity churchyard under the gaze of God, Christ and the saints.

His other locally based paintings include *The Baptism* (with Christ up to his chest in Thames water), *Christ Preaching at Cookham Regatta* and *Swan Upping at Cookham*.

More than a hundred of Spencer's paintings are on display at a small gallery in the village devoted to his work. The building was formerly a Wesleyan chapel in which the Spencer family worshipped – and *Ecstasy in a Wesleyan Chapel* is one of the paintings in the permanent collection.

And then there were those 'water cures' that were all the rage from the late 18th century into the Victorian era. Many patients flocked to spas or the seaside, so why shouldn't the Thames give a healing touch? At Sudbrook Park (now part of Richmond Golf Club) Dr James Ellis ran a hydropathy clinic which advertised the qualities of its water and the restorative effects of its riverside walks.

The Lasher pool

Weirs, with their swift currents, are dangerous places, and the one by Sandford Lock, just south of Oxford, is notorious for the number of lives it has claimed over the years.

Several university students are among those who have drowned here after being swept into the pool beneath the weir and becoming trapped under the swirling water. It's known as the Sandford Lasher.

In *Three Men in a Boat* it's described, with grim humour, as 'a very good place to drown yourself in'.

In 1846 Dr Ellis faced a manslaughter charge when one of his trusting patients died after undergoing the cold-water treatment. This was a mere blip, however; the charge was dropped, and by 1860 the establishment had such a high reputation that it attracted the rigorously scientific Charles Darwin as a client.

And the dog came too

The dreaminess of the upper Thames is well captured in a book better known for its understated English humour than for its descriptive lushness – Jerome K. Jerome's *Three Men in a Boat*, first published in 1889 and never out of print since. The trio are on a fortnight's jaunt, accompanied by the narrator's fox terrier, Montmorency.

We caught a breeze, after lunch, which took us gently up past Wargrave and Shiplake. Mellowed in the drowsy sunlight of a summer's afternoon, Wargrave, nestling where the river bends, makes a sweet old picture as you pass it, and one that lingers upon the retina of memory.

Passages such as this are a reminder that Jerome originally set out to write a guide book rather than a comic masterpiece.

> The river up to Sonning winds in and out through many islands and is very placid, hushed, and lonely. Few folk, except at twilight a pair or two of rustic lovers, walk along its banks ... It is a part of the river in which to dream of bygone days, and vanished forms and faces, and things that might have been, but are not, confound them.

> We got out at Sonning, and went for a walk round the village. It is the most fairy-like little nook on the whole river. Every house is smothered in roses, and now, in early June, they were bursting forth in clouds of dainty splendour.

Elements of that original travelogue survive among the comic episodes, and they aren't always flattering to the river – and especially not to some of the people our three friends are forced to share it with. They have a particular aversion to steamboats, which it seems are beginning to swarm.

'I never see a steam-launch', says the narrator, 'but I feel I should like to lure it to a lonely part of the river, and there, in the silence and the solitude, strangle it.'

But we're getting ahead of ourselves: we'll come to clamorous entertainment on the Thames later on. Here we'll succumb to one last, highly overblown, serenade from Jerome to the river in its serenest mood. The three are setting off from Kingston:

It was a glorious morning, late spring or early summer, as you care to take it, when the dainty sheen of grass and leaf is blushing to a deeper green; and the year seems like a fair young maid, trembling with strange, wakening pulses on the brink of womanhood.

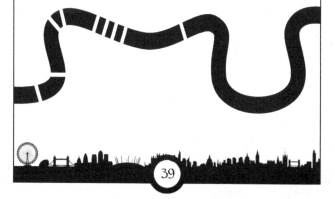

Attractions by the non-tidal Thames

Kelmscott Manor (Society of Antiquaries of London). The interior decor of William Morris's country home (*see pages 28-29*) is much as he left it, with his furniture, his books and many of his textile designs. The house is open to the public two days a week during the summer.

Cliveden (National Trust). In 1851, after two original houses on the spot had burned down, the Duke of Sutherland commissioned Sir Charles Barry, architect of the Houses of Parliament, to build the present Italianate pile. It was bought by the American billionaire William Waldorf Astor in 1893, and in the 1960s became notorious as the place where the Profumo affair played out.

Windsor Castle (The Crown). The longest occupied palace in Europe was built soon after the Norman Conquest of 1066 and has been used by the monarch since the reign of Henry I, the Conqueror's son. The Queen stays here most weekends (*tip: if the flag is flying, she's in*), plus a month at Easter and a week in June for Royal Ascot.

The castle, which is open daily, occupies 5.3 hectares (13 acres), and a great many of its magnificent interiors are open to the public, including the State Apartments created by Edward III in the 14th century: some of the rooms at the eastern end had to be restored after a devastating fire in 1992. The Long Walk in the surrounding parkland is a double-lined avenue of trees running for 4.26 km (2.65 miles).

Hampton Court (The Crown). Cardinal Wolsey had his magnificent palace built from 1515, but fell from grace and saw it seized by the man he'd served so faithfully, Henry VIII.

Henry enlarged the building, but it was given a much more substantial overhaul by William III at the end of the 17th century. He had intended to match the over-the-top grandeur of Versailles in France, and he pulled down much of the original structure, but work stopped after only a few years – leaving Hampton Court as an odd fusion of the Tudor and the baroque.

It's open daily, and has some special features: its famous maze, an historic 'real tennis' court and what's billed as the largest grapevine in the world.

'The greatest ships
that ride upon
the sea come and
unload in London
in the very harte
of the towne. '

CHAPTER TWO

AWASH WITH TRADE

The Thames has been a commercial highway ever since the Romans built their wharves downstream from London Bridge, but it takes a leap of the imagination to envisage the immense scale of traffic that almost throttled the river during the early 18th century when London had become the busiest port in the world.

Such a log-jam of tightly packed sailing ships and barges lay mid-river waiting to unload their cargoes that it was said you could cross from one bank to the other simply by stepping across their decks.

The London river had already become a bustling conduit in medieval times. Venetian galleys jostled with English trading vessels on the crowded narrow waterway, with huge quantities of wool and cloth being exported to Antwerp and Calais, and luxuries such as wine, sugar and spices coming the other way.

Elizabeth I cashed in on this prosperity by introducing a system of 'legal quays'. Goods could only be landed or loaded at officially recognised ports, where customs officers would take a cut for the Crown.

Navy HQ

There had been a ship-building and repair industry in London since Saxon times, but it was given a major boost by Henry VIII, who decided that his naval base at Portsmouth was too distant and too difficult to defend.

He anchored the fleet close to his palace at Greenwich, and the King's Yard at Deptford soon expanded to 12 ha (thirty acres), with two wet docks, three slipways and all the facilities necessary for the building, repair and servicing of warships.

This meant an end to business at a large array of 'creeks, wharves, quays, loading and discharging places' all the way up the river from Gravesend to London Bridge. Just 20 existing quays were given the official nod, all on the north bank between London Bridge and the Tower of London.

A further stipulation was that each had to specialise – in fish, corn, oil, woollen cloths, wine and so on. Bear and Young's quays, unusually, were designated for trade with Portugal because they were close to wharves used by Portuguese merchants.

The Queen also became a shareholder in the former Merchant Adventurers Company which, after a wool-for-furs trading deal with Ivan the Terrible, was renamed the Muscovy Company and granted a monopoly on English trade with Russia. The company's backers had put up a huge sum of money to send Sir Hugh Willoughby and Richard Chancellor to Moscow as negotiators: Chancellor pulled off the deal, but Willoughby was travelling in a separate ship which became trapped in the Arctic ice: he and his crew froze to death.

Fortunes as well as lives were in jeopardy during the so-called Age of Exploration, and entrepreneurs shared the risks by forming syndicates. These 'joint-stock companies' created trading posts in far-flung places and were rewarded with monopolies for trading there. The system clearly worked: in the second half of the 16th century the annual tonnage of shipping entering London rose by 50 per cent.

Gresham's gift

The pre-eminence of the City of London as a financial centre had its beginnings in the joint-stock companies formed to bolster Thames trade in Tudor England. Thomas Gresham, who as Crown agent had raised money for Elizabeth I on the Antwerp money exchange, opened a similar institution in London where the merchants could meet to transact their business.

The building opened in 1567 at the junction of Cornhill and Threadneedle Street. Four years later the Queen paid it a visit – and it was afterwards known as the Royal Exchange.

A docks revolution

An anonymous foreign traveller's account of London a little before the Great Fire praised:

the commodity of the river and boates, the prodigious bridge; the dew and dayly visit of the ebbing and flowing of the sea in the Thames, which visiting London dewly once a day, either bringeth to it or carryeth from it all merchandize the world can afford it, or it the world.

The greatest ships that ride upon the sea come and unload in London in the very harte of the towne.

By 1726, when Daniel Defoe published *A Tour Through the Whole Island of Britain*, the Thames was busier still, its heavily laden merchantmen bringing home the produce of a growing crop of overseas colonies.

'I have had the curiosity', he wrote, 'to count the ships as well as I could . . . and have found above two thousand sail of all sorts, not reckoning barges, lighters or pleasure-boats and yachts.'

Impressive it may have been, but the chock-a-block cramming of two thousand ships into a space adequate for about five hundred was bad for business. Time meant money, and a huge amount of it was being wasted. Although quays stretched 18 km (eleven miles) on both sides of the river, it was impossible for ships to unload directly onto them. They lay at anchor in midstream, and lightermen ferried the goods to and fro on their flat-bottomed barges. The whole process could take weeks.

Various ideas were put forward, including deepening the river, building a canal network and even cutting a channel through the snake-like bends between Rotherhithe and Greenwich to create large wet docks (that is, open harbours) for ocean-going vessels.

In the 1790s the traders began to get bolshy, led by the importers of sugar and rum from the West Indies who brought investors together at the Royal Exchange to form the West India Dock Company – and who threatened to take their very considerable business elsewhere if they weren't allowed to build a large tide-free dock, controlled by locks, on the Isle of Dogs.

There was no shortage of groups with vested interests who argued against the scheme, no doubt realising that it was a foretaste of revolutionary changes to the waterfront:

- Lightermen, who would no longer be needed to ferry goods to the warehouses

- Porters, car-men and the like whose work along the riverside would no longer be needed

- The owners of legal quays, whose business would dwindle

- The City of London, which argued that any infringement of urban land would fly in the face of their ancient rights and privileges

After a prolonged debate, the company won. An Act of 1799 gave it the right to create docks where custom duties could be paid (so overturning the old legal quays system), plus a 21-year monopoly on goods shipped to and from the West Indies to London. For the lightermen there was at least a little relief: under the 'free water clause' they were allowed to carry goods between the new docks and the riverside wharves free of any dues.

Heart of darkness

A substantial source of income for merchants in the port of London was the vile trade in African slaves transported to the Americas.

The merchant adventurer John Hawkins was funded by Elizabeth I among others when he set sail in 1562 on a voyage which would see him seize 300 Africans and sell them in the Spanish West Indies. The Queen had expressed the pious wish that such a thing wouldn't happen, believing that it would be 'detestable and call down the vengeance of Heaven upon the undertakers'.

Some hope! By the early 18th century 50 ships a year were leaving the Thames on these wretched expeditions, backed by money from the City of London. It's reckoned that between 1662 and 1807 – when slavery was abolished in Britain – some three million Africans were shipped to America, with another half a million dying en route.

London ships dominated the trade until the 1730s, when first Bristol and then Liverpool challenged their supremacy, and they set off on some 3,350 slaving voyages in all.

Many famous names were involved, including Sir Walter Raleigh, who went on a slaving voyage in 1567, and the diarist Samuel Pepys, who became a shareholder in the syndicate Royal Adventurers into Africa which had been granted a licence by Charles II.

In 1713, under the terms of the Treaty of Utrecht, Britain was awarded the 'asiento' – the right to carry enslaved Africans to the Spanish Americas. The government promptly sold the privilege to the South Sea Company for £7.5 million, a stupendous figure for those times, indicating the vast profits that could be made.

There were no ships freighted with manacled Africans to trouble a sensitive Londoner's conscience, but many slaves returned from the colonies with their masters (a few managing to escape), and the end-products of this officially sanctioned cruelty were obvious to anyone who watched the boats unloading.

London warehouses were heaving with vast quantities of sugar, cotton and tobacco derived from forced labour on plantations in the colonies.

South of the river

While the new tide-free locks were predominantly on the north bank of the Thames, the largest of them all was developed on the other side, opposite the Isle of Dogs.

The Surrey Commercial Docks began life as Howland Great Wet Dock at the end of the 17th century and eventually expanded to occupy 85 per cent of the Rotherhithe peninsula. Whereas the West India Docks covered 22 ha (54 acres), this enterprise (formed from a merger of two competing companies) stretched to a massive 186 ha (460 acres), with nine separate docks.

Timber was its mainstay, and the 'deal porters' who carried huge sawn planks to the top of piles sometimes 60 ft high were elite workers not expected to retain sufficient strength after the age of 40.

'Even with a hardened shoulder', reported a survey of 1928, 'the deal porter has an unenviable task. To carry over a shaking, slippery plankway a bundle of shaking, slippery planks, when a fall would almost certainly mean serious injury, is work for specialists.'

The West India Company now built two vast basins – one of 12 ha (30 acres) for imports and another of 10 ha (24 acres) for exports – flanked by nine large warehouses capable of storing a full year's supply of sugar. Some 500 ships a year nosed in and out of the locks, and the company employed a workforce of 200 labourers.

Land grabs

The new dock was indeed, as its opponents had feared, only the first of many – and the companies which built them were not only hungry for land, but some also had their eyes on areas further up the river.

The West India Company's first development was, at least, on meadowland near Greenwich, but it quickly raised cash to build another three-basin version at Wapping, just a little downstream from the Tower. These London Docks, as they were named, required the destruction of 2,000 houses and 24 'inferior streets', several businesses, the Shadwell Waterworks and part of the grounds of St John's church.

An even greater fuss was caused by the creation of the St Katharine's Docks, right on the Tower's doorstep, in 1828. For almost 600 years the ancient local hospital had been under the patronage of the reigning queen or queen consort, and an earlier attempt to build a wet dock on the site had been thwarted by the opposition of Queen Charlotte. George IV was now on the throne, his estranged wife had died – and since his spendthrift Prince Regent days, when he revamped Buckingham Palace and created a faux oriental palace down by the sea at Brighton, he had always liked refashioning things.

Down came the venerable hospital, founded by King Stephen's wife Matilda in 1147; down came the 14th-century church next door; and down came as many as 1,250 houses and tenements, displacing (they packed them in tightly in those days) 11,300 inhabitants.

Thomas Telford, the canal builder, was employed as chief engineer, and he set about developing the 5 ha (13-acre) site into a central basin leading into east and west docks that could accommodate up to 120 ships at a time.

Many locals had objected, but it was good work for 2,500 labourers. A watching Swedish engineer, Cpn A. G. Carslund, was mightily impressed:

> I frequently witnessed a thousand men and several hundred of horses employed in the operations, besides several powerful steam-engines. At the beginning of the works wheelbarrows were employed to carry away the earth, but as the excavations proceeded and became deeper, iron railways and steam-engines were substituted. The earth was conveyed into barges, carried down the river and deposited in convenient places.*

St Katharine's was a small operation by the standards of the time, and it would later merge with the London Docks a short distance downriver, but it nevertheless employed 225 permanent men and 200 'preferred' labourers, with a further 1,700 on call.

---

* It was actually carried upriver, to be deposited on marshy land at Millbank, where the builder Thomas Cubitt designed the new suburbs of Pimlico and Belgravia on the Grosvenor estate.

The new docks specialised in importing tea from India (700,000 chests a year), and wool from New Zealand and the Falkland Islands (the warehouses could hold 600,000 bales at a time), but their position close to the City encouraged them to satisfy a taste for luxuries and exotica too:

> Ostrich feathers
> Spices
> Ivory
> China
> Tortoiseshell
> Mother of Pearl
> Tallow
> Guano (as a fertiliser)

Grand designs

Practical though their buildings were, the architects of the time seemed to think of them as secular temples. Here's a contemporary account of the large tobacco and wine warehouse at the London Docks:

'The whole building stands upon an area of near five acres, covering more ground, under one roof, than any public building or undertaking, except the pyramids of Egypt.'

The age of steam

But things were changing fast on the water. Lord Byron wrote this descriptive image of the port of London in *Don Juan* a little before the opening of St Katharine's Docks:

> A mighty mass of brick, and smoke, and shipping,
> Dirty and dusty, but as wide as eye
> Could reach, with here and there a sail just skipping
> In sight, then lost amidst the forestry
> Of masts …

Masts, in short, were on their way out, because steam-powered, iron-hulled vessels were now plying the waterways. They were big beasts – and that meant the lock gates in the recent rash of tide-free docks were too small for them.

St Katharine's wasn't exactly a white elephant, but it would soon be time for new docks in deeper water downstream:

1855 Royal Victoria Dock (Plaistow Marshes)
1860s South West India Dock (Isle of Dogs)
1868 Millwall Dock
1880 Royal Albert Dock (Gallion's Reach)
1886 Tilbury Docks

The companies strove to keep up with the times. The Royal Victoria was the first dock to be lit by electricity, so allowing round-the-clock working. Railway lines along the quays allowed hydraulically-powered cranes to load cargoes directly into wagons. The Tilbury Docks relied entirely on the railway for carrying goods inland because there were as yet no roads in that wild area: 80 km (fifty miles) of sidings connected the quays to a new depot at Whitechapel.

There was no escaping the fact, though, that they were in trouble – and the East and West India Dock Company actually went into receivership. It had lost most of its old monopolies; the shipping companies played the various docks off against each other to keep berthing rates low; and ports such as Liverpool were taking away some of their business. As profits fell, investors complained about their dwindling dividends.

In 1900 a royal commission was set up to examine what had gone wrong, and its members visited other British ports and their continental counterparts such as Hamburg and Rotterdam in order to make comparisons.

Its findings were damning:

- A lack of investment meant that facilities along the Thames were outdated.
- Because of neglect by the Thames Conservancy the river was too shallow to allow ships to reach the upper docks and wharves.
- Turn-around times for loading and unloading were too slow.
- Rail connections were poor.
- Docking charges were too high.
- Divisions of responsibility had obstructed the port's improvement.

Its recommendation was that a single public authority should manage both the docks and the tidal river, from Teddington Lock down to the sea.

A new broom

And so it came about that in 1903 – to howls of protest from those who regarded it as a dangerous step towards socialism – the government proposed that the port be administered by a newly created Port of London Authority (PLA).

The Great Dock Strike

The port's labourers were a long-suffering body of men who, through a system known as the 'call-on', waited outside the dock gates in their thousands each day, and in all weathers, in the hope of being given a few hours of often dangerous work for a pittance.

Their grievances came to a head in August 1889, when the cargo ship *Lady Armstrong* was being unloaded in the West India Docks. The dockers could earn 'plus' money for turning a job round quickly, and they discovered that the company's general manager had cut the rate to attract more trade through his lock.

The men walked out, a strike committee was formed and 100,000 dockers in other parts of the port downed tools in sympathy. A new workers' union recruited large numbers of the workforce, demanding a 'dockers' tanner' – a rate of sixpence an hour – and parading in peaceful processions which made an impression on neutral observers.

One of these was the Roman Catholic Cardinal Manning, who offered himself as a mediator and was respected by both sides.

The men's unprecedented action virtually closed the port for a month, and it raised in the general public an awareness of how the lower classes were forced to survive, often in inhumane conditions.

'The poor fellows are miserably clad, scarcely with a boot on their foot, in a most miserable state', reported Colonel George Birt in evidence to a parliamentary committee – and he, remarkably, was general manager of the Millwall Dock Company.

'These are men', he went on, 'who come to work in our docks, who come on without having a bit of food in their stomachs, perhaps since the previous day. They have worked for an hour and have earned 5d. Their hunger will not allow them to continue: they take 5d in order that they may get food, perhaps the first food they have had for twenty-four hours.'

Not only was the strike successful, but it's regarded as a vital moment in the development of the Labour movement. Among those involved in the dispute was the London county councillor John Benn, who later became the first of four generations of his family to serve as MPs, including Tony and Hilary Benn.

Argument and counter-argument rattled on for years, but nationalisation of the dock companies was, indeed, the eventual outcome. In March 1909 the PLA began its work as a non-profit, self-governing trust accountable to the Board of Trade, with any profits to be used in improving facilities or reducing charges.

It took over the duties of the Thames Conservancy on the tidal river, and had a wide range of responsibilities:

- Maintenance of the river channels
- Provision of moorings
- Regulation of river traffic
- Licensing of wharves
- Towage in the docks (but not on the river)
- Removal of wrecks
- Prevention of pollution
- Registration of licensing for craft, watermen and lightermen
- Regulation of dock labour

Although the riverside wharves remained in private hands, the Authority had inherited around 1,200 ha (3,000 acres) of land, 51 km (32 miles) of quays and 17 London County Council passenger piers.

The Polish-born novelist Joseph Conrad was a sea captain who knew the Thames well. In *The Mirror of the Sea*, written at the time the Authority was being set up, he gives a vivid picture of the busy port.

> This stretch of the Thames from London Bridge to the Albert Docks is to other watersides of river ports what a virgin forest would be to a garden. It is a thing grown up, not made. It recalls a jungle by the confused, varied, and impenetrable aspect of the buildings that line the shore, not according to a planned purpose, but as if sprung up by accident from scattered seeds. Like the matted growth of bushes and creepers veiling the silent depths of an unexplored wilderness, they hide the depths of London's infinitely varied, vigorous, seething life...

A last hurrah

Although the First World War interrupted the PLA's plans, work began in 1912 on the first new dock in a generation south of the Royal Albert Dock. The George V Dock, then the most modern in the world, covering 26 ha (64 acres) and with 5 km (three miles) of quays, was opened by the king in July 1921.

The three royal quays alone now extended over 93 ha (230 acres), the world's largest surface of impounded water. During the 1930s an estimated 1,500 wharves, jetties and yards lined the Thames from Brentford to Gravesend. In 1938 some 38 per cent of the UK's trade (64 million tonnes of it) passed through the port of London and all of 50,000 ocean-going ships came up the river.

And yet – who could have seen it coming? – the end of all this profitable clamour lay just around the corner. By 1980 every dock but Tilbury had closed.

The story is swiftly told. First came the Second World War, in which German bombers inflicted massive damage on the port. (In one night alone 386,000 tonnes of timber were destroyed at the Surrey Docks.) The docks were rebuilt and trade began to recover.

And then came a transport revolution, with containers unloaded from huge ships. Deep water was essential; large numbers of labourers were not. On the London river a centuries-old way of life simply disappeared.

Docklands

Today we have London Docklands, an area encompassing the boroughs of Southwark, Tower Hamlets, Lewisham, Newham and Greenwich, and for which the watchword is 'regeneration'.

You can rejoice in green walks opened up alongside a quieter river or snarl at the brute pomp of looming skyscrapers out of scale with their surroundings. You can applaud the provision of thousands of new riverside homes or decry the gentrification of former down-to-earth, workaday communities.

Meanwhile, controversial though its lineaments may be, the colonisation of the riverside continues in a steady easterly direction. The trade has largely gone, but the shaping of the Thames is unfinished business.

❛I have witnessed such scenes of squalor and crime and suffering as oppress the mind even to a feeling of awe.❜

CHAPTER THREE

TROUBLED WATERS

There's something about being out on the river that sets people free – sometimes innocently free from the day-to-day cares of life, but all too often free from the bounds of common decency and the law. The Thames has long been known for the scurrilous behaviour of those who have worked and played on it.

It's little wonder, then, that the very first police force in the country was established here – in 1800, 30 years before Robert Peel recruited his London bobbies. The man who founded it reckoned that there were 11,000 ne'er-do-wells making a dishonest living on the water.

Blessed Trinity

Trinity House, the charity dedicated to safeguarding shipping and seafarers – and perhaps best known for maintaining lighthouses all around the British coastline – had its origins in crooked behaviour on the Thames in Tudor times.

With dishonest pilots allegedly being paid by rival merchants to run ships aground, a group of masters and mariners presented a petition to Henry VIII. In 1514 a royal charter gave responsibility for safety on the river to 'The Masters, Wardens and Assistants of the Guild or Fraternitie of the most glorious and blessed Trinities and Saint Clement in the parish Church of Deptford Stronde in the county of Kent'.

Trinity House (thank goodness they shortened the name) was to provide the safe guiding of ships along the Thames by experienced pilots. Vessels entering the port were charged a levy to pay for the service.

Elizabeth I later extended the Trinity House remit to include the provision of buoys and beacons to mark safe channels and the authorisation of Thames watermen.

This upright figure was the Scottish merchant and magistrate Patrick Colquhoun. He gave his own private Thames River Police a trial run in 1798, claiming that goods worth around £500,000 were being filched in the Pool of London every year, thanks to 'the depraved habits and loose conduct of a great proportion of the lower classes of the people'.

West India merchants were among the interested parties who funded a one-year experiment which he later claimed had been instrumental in saving cargoes worth more than £120,000.

An angry reaction from the river workers wasn't surprising, especially as many worked for very little pay in miserable conditions and relied on regular pilfering to put food in their children's mouths. A crowd of 2,000 stormed the police office, trying to burn it down, and in the subsequent skirmish one of the 50 officers was killed.

The authorities decided that Colquhoun had made his case, and the Marine Police Bill turned it from a private into a public body.

Henry Mayhew, the famous chronicler of Victorian working-class life, made a study of the docks and was staggered by what he found:

I have witnessed such scenes of squalor and crime and suffering as oppress the mind even to a feeling of awe.

Pass from the quay and warehouses to the courts and alleys that surround them, and the mind is as bewildered with the destitution of the one place, as it is with the superabundance of the other.

The very fact of being a Thames labourer was enough to give a man a bad reputation. A chaplain at Newgate prison in the 1750 said of one inmate, 'He did work upon the River. This is a very suspicious Way of Life, such People being generally looked upon as getting more Money by the bye than by their Labour'.

Sucking the monkey

The docks that warehoused alcohol frisked their labourers to make sure that they weren't taking empty bottles inside, but the desperate always found a way.

On a Friday morning in 1875 the 29-year-old labourer Thomas Collins turned up at the London Docks in good health to work in the spirit vaults, but in the evening he was discovered insensible by a workmate, and early the next morning he died.

'Deceased's wife', read a court report, 'stated that she had heard her husband speak about sucking the monkey. She knew he used a bone for that purpose.'

What Collins had been doing was inserting a mutton bone into the bung of a barrel in order to suck up raw spirit.

Poverty maps

For his *Inquiry into Life and Labour of the People in London* (1886–1903), the Victorian social reformer Charles Booth drew up colour-coded maps to show the most deprived parts of the capital.

The area around the docks was shown to be the poorest, with 35 per cent of the population suffering 'abject poverty'.

Criminal guilds

A parliamentary report of 1784 observed that as soon as ships from the East Indies arrived at their moorings 'the places near which they lie become the resort of smugglers and resemble a public fair'.

Tide-free docks gave the companies greater security, but there were always opportunities for smuggling further down the Thames where vulnerable ships lay waiting for a rising tide.

Execution Dock

A scaffold stood on the quayside at Wapping for more than 400 years, and at this so-called Execution Dock pirates, smugglers and mutineers were hanged to public gaze.

Pirates (including the notorious Captain Kidd) met a particularly horrible end. A short rope was used so as to cause a slow death by asphyxiation, the dying man's spasms being known as 'the marshal's dance'.

The last hangings here took place in 1830.

In fact there were so many kinds of illegal activity along the river that they were given names to distinguish them – almost as if their felonious practitioners were members of guilds promoting individual crafts.

Scuffle-hunters (a.k.a. **Long apron men**). Men apparently looking for work, but in fact hoping to take advantage of any disturbances to make off with goods left on the quaysides.

Light horsemen. Thieves in league with a ship's mate, boarding a West Indiaman at night to carry sugar ashore to Copemen, or receivers.

Lumpers. Employed porters and labourers making money on the side, often by throwing goods into the river at high tide for recovery by their accomplices.

Heavy horsemen. The above, but specialising in wearing concealed pouches in which to hide stolen goods.

River pirates. Armed men who cut the mooring ropes of lighters by night, allowing them to drift to banks downstream.

Night plunderers. Gangs in league with corrupt watchmen who identified unguarded vessels close by.

Mud-larks. Men apparently looking for old rope, lumps of coal and similar pickings around a ship lying at low tide, but in fact collecting goods passed to them by accomplices on board.

Dirty work

We turn to Charles Dickens to savour the dark underbelly of Thames working life. In the grim opening of *Our Mutual Friend* we see, in the dim early evening light, the 'half savage' Gaffer Hexam and his daughter Lizzie in their dirty little rowing boat with a dead body on a towline behind. Collecting cadavers is how they make their living – that and raiding their pockets for valuables.

When Lizzie shows distress about what they are doing, Gaffer asks how she can be so thankless to her 'best friend' – meaning the river. As he reminds her, they are scavengers, and the Thames has given them every little thing they possess.

The very fire that warmed you when you were a babby, was picked out of the river alongside the coal barges. The very basket that you slept in, the tide washed ashore. The very rockers that I put it upon to make a cradle of it, I cut out of a piece of wood that drifted from some ship or another.

Gaffer would have known where to take the corpse, and that was probably on the south side of the river. The authorities on the Surrey bank at that time paid twice as much as their counterparts across the water.

The hulks

In *Great Expectations* Dickens features a sorry Thames sight – the decommisioned vessels known as hulks that were first moored in the river in 1776. These were prison ships, and the convict Abel Magwitch escapes from one and surprises the terrified young Pip with a manacle still attached to his ankle.

Victorian opinion turned against the terrible conditions in these floating gaols. After the last of them, the *Defense*, was burned to a cinder in Woolwich Docks in 1857 the practice was abandoned.

Writ in water

John Taylor (1578–1653) spent most of his working life as a Thames waterman, carrying passengers across the river on his wherry, or rowing boat, at a time when only London Bridge spanned the water.

He was clerk to the watermen's guild and he spoke out against two harms inflicted on his trade: the decison by the theatre companies to move from the south bank to the north in 1612, and the development of horse-drawn carriages with sprung suspension, encouraging people to travel on the roads rather than by water.

First and foremost, though, he regarded himself as 'The Water Poet'. He was the first writer to record the death of Shakespeare in print, and he self-published around 150 works in all. As a publicity stunt he sailed down the Thames as far as the Medway in a paper boat. How on earth would he keep afloat?

> In which extremity I thought it fit
> To put in use a stratagem of wit,
> Which was, eight bullocks bladders
>   we had bought
> Puffed stiffly full with wind, bound fast
>   and taut.

While no other river trade was as vile as Gaffer's, many of them were what we would today regard as back-breaking.

The hauliers would wait for hire on the jetties and then, in large gangs, shoulder a cable weighing a tonne to tow a fully laden barge along their 'reach' of the river. When the tow-path ran out it was time to hand over to another gang on the far bank – which meant wading, perhaps chest high, into midstream.

Or consider the leggers working in canals leading off the Thames. There were no towpaths in the early tunnels, and these sturdy souls had to propel the barge by pushing their feet against the walls.

Water-language

It's not surprising that these men, their days spent in sweat and toil among other toughened denizens of the river, earned a reputation for hard drinking and rough speech. Indeed, the Oxford English Dictionary glosses 'water-language' as 'the rough language of watermen'. They seemed beyond respectability.

Men like the hauliers and leggers were a law unto themselves, but other workers were members of organisations which felt they had a reputation to keep – or to repair.

In 1701 the Corporation of Watermen banned the use of 'immoderate, obscene and lewd expressions towards passengers and each other, as are offensive to all sober persons, and tend extremely to the corruption and debauchery of youth'. Those found guilty of mouthing off were fined.

A century later, although bad language wasn't specifically mentioned, an apprentice waterman was expected to behave like (or perhaps rather better than) a gentleman: 'He shall not haunt Taverns or Play Houses, nor absent himself from his Master's Service Day or Night, unlawfully . . .'

At which point let's admit that river workers had no monopoly on ripe language. Here's Jerome K. Jerome, in *Three Men in a Boat*: 'When a man up the river thinks a thing, he says it.' The Thames spirit, in other words, was allowed to set any man's tongue free.

The Victorian nature writer Richard Jefferies, although in his books he was never tempted into the hint of a profanity, agreed. 'On the Thames,' he rejoiced, 'you may swear as the wind blows – however you list. You may begin at the mouth off the Nore and curse your way up to Cricklade. A hundred miles for swearing is a fine preserve: it is one of the marvels of civilisation.'

Naughty, naughty

For wickedness by the Thames surely nothing beats the 18th-century doings of the Hellfire Club rakes (including the artist William Hogarth and the radical politician John Wilkes) in the caves at Medmenham Abbey – or that's what its members liked to think.

What actually went on there isn't known, but the world was certainly meant to imagine pagan rites, hard drinking and wild orgies. A portrait of Sir Francis Dashwood, the club's leading light, reveals how he liked to be seen: it's a parody of a painting of St Francis of Assisi, with the Bible replaced by an erotic novel.

However accepting we may be of the habit, it seems a shame that our first mention of women workers in these pages should be to record their reputation for verbal filth. Billingsgate always had the ripest dockland reputation, and 'to swear like a fishwife' is an established expression in the English language.

Wet-erendum!

What better place to stage a political battle than on the River Thames! In June 2016, as the UK prepared for a referendum on whether to stay in the European Union, the 'Brexit' party UKIP hired a luxury cruiser, *Edwardian*, with its leader Nigel Farage on board, to be joined close to Westminster Bridge by a dozen fishing boats championing the 'Fishing for Leave' cause.

Enter the pop star, charity fundraiser and 'Remain' advocate Bob Geldof on a large pleasure boat, *Sarpedon*, which blasted loud Sixties music (including 'The In Crowd') at the rival craft. As horrified river authorities looked on, the trawlermen drenched Geldof's boat with hoses and boarded it, while inflatables from both sides recklessly weaved in and out between their mother ships.

The market women were known not only for drinking gin, taking snuff and smoking pipes of tobacco, but (the sensitive should turn the page) a 1736 dictionary defined a 'Billingsgate' as 'a scolding, impudent slut'.

As an immediate corrective, though, we should note that in 1805 the cartoonist Cruikshank, in his 'A New Catamaran Expedition', chose to shame the prime minister, Pitt the Younger, into taking military action by depicting a fleet of Billingsgate fishwives sailing across the Channel to terrorise the French.

It's high time we met them . . .

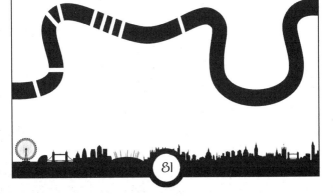

'They are not polite at Billingsgate, as all the world knows, and "by your leave" is only a preliminary to your hat being knocked off your head by a bushel of oysters or a basket of crabs.'

CHAPTER FOUR

'ALIVE, ALIVE~O!'

Accounts of Billingsgate market in its Victorian heyday thrill to the vibrant bustle of the place, echoing with street cries from the early hours, its slabs piled high with trays of fish, the air heavy with the smell of the sea.

Porters in leather helmets (or 'bobbing hats') hurry by with laden trolleys, those fishwives with their baskets utter a few choice words, the merchants do deals with the middlemen known as bummarees, who then sell on to that army of street traders, the canny, raucous, much maligned costermongers.

The costermonger characteristically wore a small cloth cap, jauntily set to one side, a corduroy waistcoat, a large, brightly coloured silk cravat (known as the Kingsman) and trousers tight at the knee and flaring down to the feet.

Nobody seems to have thought much of this hard-working tribe. In *Henry IV, part 2*, Shakespeare has Falstaff lament 'Virtue is of so little regard in these costermonger times'.

Henry Mayhew made a close study of them in his book about the London poor. Up to 4,000 worked each day at Billingsgate, and here are a few of his findings:

Only about one in ten of the regular costermongers is able to read.

The costermonger's love of a good strong boot is a singular prejudice that runs throughout the whole class.

The costermongers, taken as a body, entertain the most imperfect idea of the sanctity of marriage. To their undeveloped minds it merely consists in the fact of a man and woman living together.

On the other hand, he quotes a leading salesman as saying he would rather take an order from a costermonger than a fishmonger, 'for the one paid ready money, while the other required credit'.

Some traders disliked the way Mayhew wrote about them, and in 1851 they established a Street Traders' Protection Association as a form of self defence. Goodness knows what they would have made of the American novelist Nathaniel Hawthorne's nose-in-the-air opinions written six years later, but published (as *English Notebooks*) only after his death:

> Yesterday we went to London Bridge and Lower Thames Street, and quickly found ourselves in Billingsgate Market – a dirty, evil smelling, crowded precinct, thronged with people carrying fish on their heads, and lined with fish-shops and fish-stalls, and pervaded with a fishy odour. The footwalk was narrow – as indeed was the whole street – and filthy to travel upon; and we had to elbow our way among rough men and slatternly women, and to guard our heads from the contact of fish-trays.

Very ugly, grimy and misty, moreover, is Billingsgate Market, and though we heard none of the foul language of which it is supposed to be the fountain-head, yet it has its own peculiarities of behaviour. For instance, U. tells me that one man, staring at her and her governess as they passed, cried out, 'What beauties!' – another, looking under her veil, greeted her with 'Good morning, my love!' We were in advance, and heard nothing of these civilities.

Another contemporary observer, Dr Andrew Wynter, while marvelling at the way that half of the capital's fish supply was hurried across the land by night to meet the five o'clock opening time, added a warning:

Let the visitor beware how he enters the market in a good coat, for, as sure as he goes in in broad cloth, he will come out in scale armour. They are not polite at Billingsgate, as all the world knows, and 'by your leave' is only a preliminary to your hat being knocked off your head by a bushel of oysters or a basket of crabs.

A teeming river

By the time Billingsgate was established as a fish market in the 16th and 17th centuries (it was officially recognised by an Act of Parliament in 1699), the river by which it stood had been putting food on local tables for at least a thousand years.

Archaeologists have found the remains of several Anglo-Saxon fish traps in the Thames, and they can still be seen at very low tides. The two best preserved are at Isleworth (dated AD 650–890) and Chelsea (AD 730–900), and there are even earlier examples at Putney, Hammersmith and Vauxhall.

The traps were made from pliable willow 'withies' held in place on the riverbed by stout posts, and were fashioned in a V-shape so that trapped fish could be held in the long neck. Since the Isleworth trap has its opening facing downstream while the one at Chelsea faces upstream, it's thought that they were designed to catch different kinds of fish: perhaps eels coming downstream in the one, and salmon swimming upstream in the other.

Accounts from the medieval period testify to a river well stocked with fish. Although William Harrison, writing in the 16th century, condemned a trend towards overfishing with nets, he licked his lips to think of 'the fat and sweet salmons, dailie taken in this streame', and added a list of other species, including barbel, trout, perch, roach, smelt, dace and gudgeon.

Smelt was regarded as a delicacy, and the trade was profitable. Fishermen would put their sons to work at the age of nine for a seven-year apprenticeship. They stretched a net between two peterboats – double-ended boats about 3.7m (12 feet) in length and containing a well for live fish – and each haul of the net might bring up 3,000 of them. Billingsgate was selling 50,000 a day in 1810.

The eel-like lampreys were also in great demand. Edward Ironside, in his *History and Antiquities of Twickenham*, published in 1797, tells us a small variety known as lamperns were caught locally between November and June, and 'used as baits by the English and Dutch in the cod and turbot fishery. Large quantities are fetched by the Hollanders from the Thames.'

Many miles of banks upstream from Staines to Cricklade were once honeycombed below water level with the holes, or 'boles', that were home to crayfish, close relatives of lobsters. The making of crayfish pots was a prosperous industry in the Oxford area, and a dish of these freshwater crustaceans – bright red when cooked – would often appear in college dining rooms.

fishermen's tale 1

A large bowhead (or Greenland) whale was caught off Greenwich in June 1658, attracting huge crowds. The diarist John Evelyn records that it appeared at low water, 'for at high water it would have destroyed all the boats'.

It was harpooned, 'and after a horrid grone' it ran ashore and died.

'Its length was 8 foote, heighth 16; black skinned like coach leather, very small eyes, greate taile, onely two small finns, a picked snout, and a mouth so wide that divers men might have stood upright in it, no teeth, and a throate yet so narrow as would not have admitted the least of fishes.'

Catching crayfish individually was something of a profitable sport for local boys, who would trim willow wands into nooses and lower them over the claws that protruded from the boles in order to catch passing prey. Another method was to insert a gloved finger into the claws and, when they closed and tugged, wrestle the aggressive creatures out and into a waiting basket.

fishermen's tale 2

In January 1787 fishermen pulled into their boat off Poplar a huge shark which was found to have a silver watch and metal chain lodged in its gut, along with a cornelian seal and fragments of gold lace. The watch bore the maker's name (Henry Warson, London) and a distinguishing number, 1369. Warson reported that Ephraim Thompson of Whitechapel had bought it from him as a present for his son, who had been bound abroad on the ship *Polly*.

It transpired that young Thompson had fallen overboard off Falmouth in a squall and was never seen again. His father bought the shark in order to preserve it as a strange memorial.

Jellied heaven

Eels were for generations part of the staple diet of working class Londoners. The tiny elvers would arrive in May after a 5,000 km (3,000-mile) journey from the Sargasso Sea, near the Bahamas. After swimming up the Thames, they would eventually grow to around 1 m (3 ft) long in their new freshwater surroundings, before returning to the Atlantic some years later to spawn and die.

They were netted in vast numbers. The first eel, pie and mash houses opened in London in the 18th century. By the end of the Second World War there were reckoned to be about a hundred of them (few survive today), their speciality being 'jellied' eels, eaten cold.*

* *'Take a large Eel, split it, and take out the Bone, and wash it; then strew it with Cloves, Mace and beaten Pepper, with Salt and sweet Herbs; then roll it up, and tye it with Splinters round it; so boil it in Water and a little Salt, and White-wine Vinegar, and a Blade of Mace; when the Eel is boil'd, take it up and let the Pickle boil a little; and when 'tis cold, put in the Eel.' – Court Cookery, 1725*

Jellied eel salesmen may not have had as bad a reputation as costermongers, but the humorist P. G. Wodehouse uses them as the butt of snobbish wit in several of his novels. One of his characters, typically, is horrified to find that an unknown man is about to marry her daughter:

'I sent for him immediately and found him to be quite impossible. He jellies eels!'
'Does what?'
'He is an assistant at a jellied eel shop.'

Eel Pie Island

This amusingly named eyot at Twickenham, reached by boat or a footbridge, was a major music venue in the 1960s. A Kingston junk-shop owner, Arthur Chisnall, organised events in a dilapidated hotel on the island (since destroyed by fire) that attracted top jazz names (Ken Colyer, Kenny Ball, George Melley, Acker Bilk), rhythm & blues bands such as the Yardbirds and rock bands the Rolling Stones and The Who.

Revellers were issued with 'Eelpiland' passports which have now become collectors' items.

Net profits

The scale of the trade is scarcely believable today, but this is Henry Mayhew's contemporary assessment of the annual turnover at Billingsgate market in the 1860s:

Salmon .. 29,000 boxes, 7 in a box
Cod, live .. 400,000, averaging 10 lb each
  barrelled .. 15,000 barrels, 50 to a barrel
  salted .. 1,600,000, averaging 5 lb each
Haddocks .. 2,470,000, at 2 lb each
Sole .. 97,520,000, at ¼ lb each
Mackerel .. 23,620,000, at 1 lb each
Herrings .. 250,000 barrels, at 150 oz each
Bloaters .. 265,000 baskets, at 150 oz each
Eels .. 9,000,000, at 6 oz to 1 lb
Whiting .. 17,920,000, at 6 oz each
Plaice .. 36,600,000, at 1 lb each
Turbot .. 800,000, at 7 lb each
Brill & Mullet .. 1,220,000, at 3 lb each
Oysters .. 500,000,000
Crabs .. 600,000
Lobsters .. 1,200,000
Prawns .. 12 tons, at 120 oz to 1 lb
Shrimps .. 192,295 gallons, at 329 to a pint

In his *Curiosities of London*, published in 1867, John Timbs consults a 'learned authority' whose tally broadly agrees with Mayhew's, and who 'startled us with such quantities as fifty million mussels, seventy million cockles, three hundred million periwinkles, five hundred million shrimps and twelve hundred million herrings'.

In short ... he told us that about four thousand million fish, weighing a quarter of a million tons, and bringing two million sterling, were sold annually at Billingsgate!

Choked to death

Of course the Thames was never the main contributor to the Billingsgate trade. In earlier times fish had arrived on ships from far-flung ports and by carriage from the southern and western parts of the country. In the Victorian era, when the market was the biggest of its kind in the world, the railway network added a new, and faster, method of supply.

Billingsgate could thrive without the Thames – and that was just as well.

A fishing elite

The Worshipful Company of Fishmongers, its headquarters overlooking the Thames at London Bridge, is ranked fourth among the 110 livery companies of the City of London. Its responsibilities include overseeing the quality of fish imported into the City, mostly via Billingsgate.

Edward I granted its first charter around 1272, with a monopoly on selling fish that lasted until the 15th century. In 1444 Fishmongers' Hall, built on land between Thames Street and the river, became the first of 40 livery halls to be caught up in the Great Fire of 1666.

Christopher Wren, who designed St Paul's Cathedral, was the architect of a new building, but it lasted only until 1828 when part of the site was cut off to make way for the new London Bridge. Its impressive replacement, in Portland stone and granite, was completed in 1835 – and was later restored after suffering heavy damage from German bombing raids in the Second World War.

The wharf, once privately owned, is now part of the public pedestrian quay.

A new home...

Until 1850, when the City architect J. B. Bunning designed a new market, Billingsgate consisted of a collection of wooden buildings – large houses around a piazza, together with a large scattering of low booths and sheds. As business continued to grow, however, a larger area was needed, and in 1877 the splendid Italianate-style confection fashioned by Sir Horace Jones rose in its place by the Thames.

That building survives as an architectural delight of the City, but in 1982 the market itself was relocated downstream to the Isle of Dogs. The City of London pays an annual rent for the site – 'the gift of one fish'.

... and a sad farewell

In April 2012, after a bitter dispute, licences were withdrawn from the porters who had for centuries enjoyed a monopoly on moving fish around the market. Modernisers accused them of operating a 'closed shop'.

Their ancient rights and practices were swept away overnight, and they were replaced by cheaper casual labour.

At the very moment when Billingsgate was heaving with the most staggering scaly harvest in its long history, the river itself was rapidly dying.

It was, in short, a cesspit – and no fish could possibly live in it.

'a Stygian pool,
reeking with
ineffable and
intolerable horrors'

CHAPTER FIVE

ONE VAST GUTTER

P oets have written so often and so evocatively about the delights of the 'silvery' Thames that an innocent reader might imagine the waters to have run bright and pure since the dawn of history.

The grim fact is that the communities along its banks treated it as a handy sewer. As London grew in size, so the river filled with filth too substantial for the tides to flush away. By 1857 *The Oarsman's Guide* was describing it as 'a sludgy compromise between the animal, the vegetable and the mineral kingdoms', while a year later *Punch* magazine declared it to be 'one vast gutter'.

But before we condemn the Victorians for their disgusting habits, we should acknowledge that they were by no means the first to foul the precious waters of life lapping at their feet.

- Archaeologists have discovered wooden soil pipes under the Roman settlement in the Cannon Street area which show that the Thames was being used as a latrine all of 2,000 years ago.

- In 1357 Edward III condemned the steady accumulations of 'dung and other filth' on the banks, and the 'fumes and other abominable stenches arising therefrom'.

Side by Side

'Dick' Whittington, the famous four-times Lord Mayor of London, created a great 'longhouse', or public lavatory, at Cheapside in the 1420s.

With 128 segregated seats (half for men and half for women) it was built over a long dock flushed twice a day by the tidal Thames. It was in use for well over 200 years until destroyed in the Great Fire of London.

- A 1535 Act of Parliament attempted to protect the river, where 'till now of late divers evil disposed persons have habitually cast in dung and filth'.

Grimy rhymes

Some poets at least forsook the pastoral mode in order to paint the river in its true, murky colours. In 1644 John Taylor (see page 76) was charged with keeping the Thames clean upstream at Oxford, where human waste was only one source of contamination:

> Dead Hogges, Dogges, Cats, and well flayd
> Carryon Horses,
> Their noysom Corpes soyld the Waters Courses;
> Both Swines and Stable dunge, Beast-guts and
> Garbage,
> Street-dust, with Gardners weeds and Rotten
> Herbage.

Alexander Pope's *Dunciad* (1728) takes us:

> To where Fleet-ditch with disemboguing streams
> Rolls the large tribute of dead dogs to Thames,
> The King of dykes! than whom no sluice of mud
> With deeper sable blots the silver flood.

And here's Tobias Smollett in his picaresque novel *The Expedition of Humphry Clinker*, published in 1771:

> If I would drink water, I must quaff the mawkish contents of an open aqueduct, exposed to all manner of defilement, or swallow that which comes from the river Thames, impregnated with all the filth of London and Westminster. Human excrement is the least offensive part of the concrete, which is composed of all the drugs, minerals and poisons used in mechanics and manufactures, enriched with the putrefying carcasses of beasts and men, and mixed with the scourings of all the wash-tubs, kennels, and common sewers within the bills of mortality.

'He who drinks a tumbler of London water', the English clergyman and wit Sydney Smith wrote in 1834, 'has literally in his stomach more animated beings than there are men, women and children on the face of the globe'.

This was two years after the first of four cholera outbreaks in the capital (the later epidemics were in 1849, 1854 and 1865) which would between them claim close on 40,000 lives.

The Great Stink

By the early Victorian period the population of London had risen to some 3 million, and the waste matter of slaughterhouses, factories and processing industries poured into a river the banks of which were packed 150 mm (six inches) deep with excrement right up to the tidal limit at Teddington.

In July 1855 (as he explained in a forthright letter to *The Times*), the scientist Michael Faraday dropped pieces of white paper into the Thames to test how opaque the water was. 'Near the bridges', he wrote, 'the feculence [filthy matter] rolled up in clouds so dense that they were visible at the surface. The smell was very bad . . . Surely the river which flows for so many miles through London ought not to be allowed to become a fermenting sewer.'

He went on to make a strikingly accurate prediction: 'If we neglect this subject, we cannot expect to do so with impunity; nor ought we to be surprised if, ere many years are over, a hot season give us sad proof of the folly of our carelessness.'

The moment of truth arrived during a spell of baking weather in 1858. The stench of untreated human waste and industrial effluent became so sickeningly powerful throughout that long summer that a name was given to it – the Great Stink.

- In June temperatures in the shade averaged 35 ℃ (95 ℉), with a top temperature of 48 ℃ (118 ℉), and as the level of the Thames fell, raw effluent from the sewers lay exposed on the banks.

- To smother the smell, hundreds of tons of lime were deposited on the foreshore at low tide and at the mouths of sewers discharging into the Thames.

- Drapes soaked in lime chloride were hung across the windows of Parliament, but even so the Chancellor of the Exchequer, Benjamin Disraeli, was seen to rush from a committee room, bent double and with a handkerchief pressed to his nose, to escape 'the pestilential odour'.

- Queen Victoria and Prince Albert, having bravely set out on a pleasure cruise along the river, turned back after only a few minutes because of the unbearable stench.

'Gentility of speech is at an end', trumpeted the City Press. 'It stinks, and whoso once inhales the stink can never forget it and can count himself lucky if he lives to remember it.'

'We can colonise the remotest ends of the earth', fulminated the *Illustrated London News*, 'we can conquer India; we can pay the interest of the most enormous debt ever contracted; we can spread our name, and our fame, and our fructifying wealth to every part of the world; but we cannot clean the River Thames.'

Something in the air

It was a common belief of the time that cholera and other diseases were caused by 'miasma' – not water-borne germs but evil-smelling air. When the social reformer Edwin Chadwick was put in charge of the London sewers in 1848 he had them regularly flushed to reduce the deadly pong – thereby sending even more human waste into the Thames.

The upside to this erroneous theory was that the Great Stink of 1858 prompted the authorities to introduce measures that were genuinely good for public health.

Of course the Victorians could do something about it. Disraeli, not permanently put out of action by the stench, tabled a bill amending the existing law governing sewers. In the debate that followed (he was a novelist, too) he memorably described the Thames as 'a Stygian pool, reeking with ineffable and intolerable horrors'.

The bill was passed into law that August. As *The Times* commented, 'Parliament was all but compelled to legislate upon the great London nuisance by the force of sheer stench'.

Dirty work

So-called 'flushermen' wearing long blue overcoats and thigh-length waders were employed to clear blockages in London's ancient sewers – but they weren't alone in their foul-smelling tunnels.

'Toshers' (sometimes whole families of them) made a living from scavenging among the filth for anything of value. Entering the sewers was prohibited in 1840, but many men carried on with their work, infiltrating the system from the shoreline with lanterns at night.

St Bazalgette

Joseph Bazalgette is the man revered almost to the point of saintliness for his major revamp of the London sewer system, thereby cleaning up the Thames and saving unnumbered thousands from bacterial diseases.

Fewer know that he was also responsible for London's handsome embankments (under which his sewers still run), or that he also designed several of the capital's bridges.

Balzagette had been appointed chief engineer of the Metropolitan Board of Works in 1856. Once the Great Stink forced a change in the law, he set about building 1,800 km (1,100 miles) of local sewers to gather up all the raw sewage, horse manure and refuse that littered the streets and alleys of the capital. Their output disgorged into 132 km (82 miles) of capacious 'intercepting' brick sewers and was pumped a few kilometres downstream to huge collecting tanks at Barking, to the north of the river, and Crossness to the south – from where it was discharged into the river, untreated, at high tide.

Ill met by moonlight

The story of the worst boating disaster in Thames history – the sinking of the paddle steamer *Princess Alice* on the evening of 3 September, 1878 with the loss of more than 600 lives – owes something of its horror to the operation of Bazalgette's new sewer system.

Overloaded with passengers enjoying a 'moonlight trip' at two shillings a head, she was on her way back from Gravesend to Swan Pier near London Bridge when she collided with the much larger SS *Bywell Castle* (a collier bound for Newcastle) close to Woolwich Pier.

The *Princess Alice* was struck on her starboard side, broke in two and sank within four minutes. Although the crews of the *Bywell Castle* and some small local craft managed to rescue 69 passengers, many were trapped on board, later found standing erect because they were so tightly packed together.

Just an hour before the collision Bazalgette's impressive sewer outfalls at nearby Barking and Crossness had discharged one of their twice-daily releases of 340,000 m³ (75 million imperial gallons) of raw sewage.

A contemporary account in *The Times* reveals what that meant for those who attempted to swim for the shore: 'The flood gates of the outfalls are opened, when there is projected into the river two continuous columns of decomposed fermenting sewage, hissing like soda water with baneful gases so black that the water is stained for miles and discharging a corrupt charnel house odour.'

It was reported two weeks later that 16 of the rescued passengers had since died, while many more were in 'a precarious state'. They had presumably been overcome by the poisonous filth in which they had struggled.

While a Board of Trade inquiry blamed the captain of the *Princess Alice* for the disaster, the jury of the coroner's inquest – and the press – found fault with the *Bywell Castle*'s captain, too.

The tragedy shamed the authorities into action. A royal commission recommended that solid matter in the sewage should be separated out before discharge. Sludge was carried off by steam boats and dumped out in the estuary.

The marine police force at Wapping had its rowing boats replaced by steam launches to enable a swifter response to accidents.

The renowned Victorian energy is epitomised by the speed at which this huge enterprise was undertaken. The system was officially opened by the Prince of Wales in 1865 – six years after work began – and the whole project was fully completed within another ten.

Bazalgette was foresighted. Knowing there would never be another chance to remodel the city so drastically, he calculated the pipe sizes needed to cope with the current sewage output and then doubled them.

That's why his honeycomb of sewers is still in use today!

Arise, Sir Joseph

Joseph Bazalgette (1819–1889) was knighted in 1874 on the completion of his prodigious achievement in creating London's sewer network and the Thames embankments.

A monument was raised to him in the Victoria Embankment gardens ten years after his death. The inscription reads 'Flumini vincula posuit' – 'He confined the river'.

Taming the river

Sir Christopher Wren had first proposed embanking the Thames after the Great Fire of London. Two hundred years later his dream was realised – and on a vast scale.

The Victoria Embankment, running between the Palace of Westminster and Blackfriars Bridge, reclaimed almost 9 ha (22 acres) of the waterway and entailed the purchase and destruction of a long stretch of wharves, warehouses and private homes. Large blocks of granite were shipped up the Thames from Cornwall for the facings, and the grand new thoroughfare covered not only Bazalgette's wide intercepting sewers but a section of the Metropolitan District Underground Railway.

The Albert Embankment, across the river from Parliament between Westminster Bridge and Vauxhall, was equally destructive of the old Thames frontages. Sepia photographs give these a rough glamour today, but the author of *Old and New London*, published a few years after they had been swept away, only rejoiced to be rid of the former 'slimy foreshore'.

He wrote of its 'hideous aspect . . . overladen as it was with dank tenements, rotten wharves and dirty boat-houses'.

The Chelsea Embankment, from Millbank to Battersea Bridge, completed the set. The chairman of the Metropolitan Board of Works, John Thwaites, was in no doubt that the embankments were a feather in London's cap: they had, he said, created 'the appropriate, and appropriately civilised, cityscape for a prosperous commercial society'.

A hymn to engineering

The Victorians valued engineering, however humble the task it had to perform, and the Crossness sewage pumping station has been described by the architectural historian Nikolaus Pevsner not only as a masterpiece of its kind, but 'a Victorian cathedral of ironwork'.

The beautiful Grade I listed building, complete with its four huge beam engines, has been restored by volunteers thanks to a £2.7 million grant from the Heritage Lottery Fund – and it's now open to the public.

'Super Sewer'

The days of the Great Stink are long gone, but today the Thames has a pollution problem all over again. With a population of around 8 million, London produces vast amounts of waste. In an average year 39 million tonnes (38 million tons) of raw sewage discharges into the river, and in 2013 adverse weather conditions sent that figure soaring to 55 million tonnes (54 million tons) – or, as Thames Water put it, the equivalent of the flushing of 8 billion toilets.

Bazalgette's mighty network has served well for around 150 years but has at last been found wanting. In 2016 work began on the 25 km (15-mile) Thames Tideway Tunnel, with six tunnel-boring machines expected to take seven years burrowing below the river from Acton in the west to Abbey Mills in the east.

'I find it embarrassing', the chair of the river charity Thames 21 has said (echoing her exasperated Victorian forebears), 'that as a first-world nation we pour our effluent into the river as if we don't have the understanding of what harm it can do.'

Ill treatment

In March 2017 Thames Water was fined a record £20.3 million for allowing 1.4 billion litres (about 3 billion pints) of raw sewage to escape from treatment works in Oxfordshire and Buckinghamshire. It leaked into the Thames and its tributaries, and also onto the Thames Path – making people and animals ill and killing more than 10,000 fish.

A monster fatberg

They're no longer called flushermen, but Thames Water staff are still employed to clear blocked sewers. In September 2017 the company discovered a vast 'fatberg' blocking tunnels below Whitechapel. This congealed mass of fat, nappies and wet wipes was estimated to weigh 130 tonnes (120 tons) and stretch for 250 m (800 ft).

A team of eight workmen, wearing protective suits and armed with shovels and high-powered jets, took three weeks to break it up. It was such a vile wonder that a section of what the company described as 'a total monster' was preserved to go on permanent display at the Museum of London.

The chief executive of the company building the so-called super sewer has likewise spoken of 'this archaic problem', but has made an optimistic claim: 'If the tunnel had been in operation last year, it would have captured 97 per cent of the sewage that poured into London's river.'

6...that great sea-flood
came widely throughout
this country, and ran
further inland than
it ever did before,
and drowned many
settlements and a
countless number of
human beings. 9

CHAPTER SIX

'WATER'S OVER!'

O n a calm day, with the sun dancing on its gentle ripples, it's hard to imagine the Thames as a source of danger, but the records show that time and again over the centuries it has swept ashore in torrents, swallowing everything in its path. The traditional warning cry was 'Water's over!'

Some accounts have a comical aspect, at least with hindsight. In 1579 the great hall at Westminster (the oldest part of our present Parliament) was so deeply awash from the melt of a violent snowstorm that the receding waters left behind a harvest of floundering fish 'for who so list [wished] to gather up'.

Westminster Hall had a long history of inundations. During the terrible storm of November 1236, the chronicler John Stow tells us, 'the river of Thames overflowing the banks, caused the marshes about Woolwitch [sic] to be all on a sea, wherein boats and other vessels were carried in the stream; so that beside cattle, the greatest number of men, women and children, inhabitants there, were drowned'.

There's no mention of fish on this occasion, but 'in the great palace of Westminster men did row with wherries [small Thames boats] in the midst of the hall, being forced to ride to their chambers'.

Suffering Saxons

The great Thames flood of 1014 is one of the earliest on record.

'In this year on St Michael's Eve', reads the *Anglo Saxon Chronicle*, 'that great sea-flood came widely throughout this country, and ran further inland than it ever did before, and drowned many settlements and a countless number of human beings.'

The historical record is littered with tales of the Thames's bad behaviour:

- 1593 After a thaw (a recurrent cause of flooding) Christchurch Meadow at Oxford lies 13 ft deep in water.

- 1663 Samuel Pepys' diary for December 7:
  'Up betimes, and, it being a frosty morning, walked on foot to White Hall ... I hear and find that there was the last night the greatest tide that ever was remembered in England to have been in this river: all White Hall having been drowned, of which there was great discourse.'

- 1763 All the meadows by the Thames, from the source to the sea, are flooded.

- 1774 The ancient wooden bridge at Henley is swept away. 'The Thames is as broad as your Danube', Horace Walpole writes from Twickenham to a friend.

- 1809 Floods destroy several bridges over the river. One is at Eton, which leaves George III stranded at Windsor.

- 1850 Rising waters extinguish the furnaces of the Wandsworth gasworks, plunging the local neighbourhood into darkness.

- **1852** The Duke of Wellington's funeral hearse, on its way from his Kent home to his state funeral in London, is overturned by flood waters after two solid weeks of rain.

- **1894** One of the worst Thames floods on record. Many locks along the river record the height of the floodwater that November – at Molesey a full 2.6m (8 feet in) above the summer average.

- **1928** A horror, in which the Thames overtops the Victorian defences and part of the Chelsea Embankment collapses. Fourteen people drown in the basements of Westminster, and thousands are left homeless.

- **1947** A national, rather than a local disaster, with massive snowfalls followed by a thaw and heavy rain falling on bone-hard ground. Most of the Thames Valley is under water, and the borough engineer at Windsor says, 'We could only cope if we had a spare Thames or two.'

- **1953** Counties facing the North Sea bear the brunt of a vicious 'storm tide' which also ravages Scotland, Belgium and the Netherlands. Hundreds are killed and tens of thousands evacuated. Giant waves surge up the Thames Estuary, drowning Canvey Island, where 83 people die.

Playing Canute

King Canute, we're told, didn't really believe he could control the waves he ordered to retreat. He was simply making a point about the futility of trying to do so – in which case he may prove to have been wiser than we are.

freaks of nature

Freak tides can cause flooding, and a notable example appears in a pamphlet of 1641 which reported two tides within the space of an hour and a half at London Bridge – 'the last comming with such violence and hideous noyse that it not onely affrighted but even astonished above 500 watermen that stood beholding it on both side of the Thames'. The river stopped moving for more than an hour, appearing to be 'asleepe or dead'.

A very different phenomenon was experienced in 1716, when 'a violent storm of wind' held the tide back. The river was so effectively drained that 'many thousands of people passed it on foot, both above and below the bridge, and walked through most of the arches'.

The Thames Barrier, which opened in 1982 and spans 520 m (1,700 ft) of the river near Woolwich, is a heroic enterprise. Modern technology's answer to the ever-rising water table, it has ten mighty steel gates which, once hydraulically set in motion, are rotated upwards* from the bed of the river to form a solid wall the height of a five-storey building.

It protects 125 km² (48 square miles) of the capital from tidal surges: in 2014, after a period of heavy rain and high tides, the Environment Agency produced a map showing large areas of London (including Parliament) that would have flooded had the barrier not been raised.

So far, so good. But London is sinking at the rate of 20 cm (8 inches) each century and the incoming tides are forecast to rise by around 0.6 m (2 ft) over the same period.

---

* The barrier's designer, Charles Draper, said he got the rotating idea from the taps on his gas cooker at home.

The original expectation was that the barrier would be used two or three times a year. The average is already between six and seven, and there have been some alarming spikes – it was raised all of 50 times during 2013–14.

Although it was designed to last until 2030, and the Environment Agency has said it doesn't envisage replacing it before 2070, some experts have warned that the clock is ticking. One proposal is for a new barrier further downriver between East Tilbury in Essex and Cliffe in Kent, while a group of academics has dreamed up an impressive structure stretching for 16 km (10 miles) across the Thames Estuary from Sheerness to Southend in Essex.

Time and tide, the adage has it, wait for no man...

123

❛ London Bridge was made for wise men to go over and fools to go under. ❜

CHAPTER SEVEN

SHORE
TO SHORE

B ack in 1671, when London Bridge was the capital's only permanent way across the river, a group of entrepreneurs had the idea of building a new one a little further west to link Fulham with Putney. The idea got as far as Parliament, where it was promptly thrown out.

Who opposed it? The City of London, which made a killing from charging tolls on the existing structure, and the Thames watermen who manned the ferries and reckoned that 60,000 of their jobs were at stake. It wasn't until 1726 that a 26-arch timber structure at last got the go-ahead – and after that there was simply no stopping the bridge builders.

for the record

The first bridge over the Thames was built by the Romans in London around AD 50.

The oldest bridge over the river today is **New Bridge**, a two-arched, 13th-century stone construction carrying the A415 across the Thames between Abingdon and Witney in Oxfordshire.

Radcot Bridge, also in Oxfordshire and carrying the A4095, is older still, dating from around 1200 – but thanks to a canal cut in 1787 it now spans a backwater.

The lowest headroom on the navigable Thames is afforded by **Osney Bridge** – carrying the A420 from Botley to Oxford – at just (2.3 m) 7 ft 6 inches.

Kingston Bridge gives the greatest headroom – excluding railway and motorway bridges – at 7.29 m (23 ft 11 inches).

And which Thames bridge did the art historian Horace Walpole describe as 'the most beautiful in the world after the Ponti di Triniti at Florence'? (See the foot of page 129 for the answer!)

By the end of the century there were new bridges at Westminster, Blackfriars, Battersea and Richmond, and the 19th century was to see a veritable rash of them.

Crossing the Thames in earlier times could be a frustrating business. A wherryman pulled on his oars, but the so-called horse ferries* (that is, large enough to take a horse and carriage) were cumbersome barges that needed to be poled from bank to bank. The water was often too deep for this at high tide, and the current could be treacherous mid-stream, so there might be a long wait for favourable conditions.

Legend has it that Putney Bridge was actively promoted by the de facto prime minister, Sir Robert Walpole, after being angered by a drunken ferryman who left him stranded on the bank.

The early bridges were private enterprises, raising money through tolls – and compensation was paid to the people whose livelihoods they damaged.

* *Horseferry Road by Lambeth Bridge is named after the one which crossed the river there.*

In the case of Putney Bridge this entailed payments to the Bishop of London and the Duchess of Marlborough, who had both profited from the ferry, plus an annual sum to the widows and children of the local watermen.

Eventually, though, this kind of arrangement was seen as out of keeping with the needs of a busy mercantile city. In 1877 a law was passed giving the Metropolitan Board of Works permission to buy all the bridges from Hammersmith to Waterloo, at the same time abolishing their tolls.

Lover's leap

In 1795, unhappy in love, the 36-year-old feminist writer Mary Wollstonecraft threw herself from Putney Bridge in a (second) suicide attempt. She failed to sink and was saved by two watermen.

Within two years she had married the political philosopher William Godwin. In August 1797 she gave birth to their daughter, Mary – later the wife of the poet Shelley and the author of *Frankenstein* – but died soon afterwards from labour complications.

It bought Putney Bridge two years later, and had Joseph Bazalgette design a handsome new five-span replacement in stone and Cornish granite, with two of his five outfall sewers incorporated in the new embankment created alongside it.

Let's take a quick hop along the bridges downstream from Putney.

The first **Wandsworth Bridge**, built in 1873, proved a flop. Investors thought a railway terminus was about to be built on the north bank, but that never happened, and within seven years the bridge was taken into public ownership. Added to that, it was too weak to carry buses, so it was knocked down and replaced during the last war by today's steel cantilever bridge. It's been unkindly described as 'the least noteworthy bridge in London', but do note its colour: that dull blue was camouflage against German air raids.

- Which bridge (see page 126) was described by Horace Walpole as the second most beautiful in the world? Henley Bridge, which carries the Thames Path over the river.

In the 1760s a ferry operated across the river where **Battersea Bridge** now stands. It was owned by the first Earl Spencer, who applied for permission to build a timber toll bridge on the spot. Until Joseph Bazalgette's 1890 replacement (iron girders on granite piers) this was the last surviving wooden bridge over the Thames in London, and it features in paintings by artists such as Turner and Whistler.

A distinguishing feature of the handsome **Albert Bridge** is its rigid 'cable-stayed' design, which soon proved to be structurally unsound. Some ten years after its 1873 opening Bazalgette improved it, and another 90 years on, the Greater London Council added two concrete piers to make it stronger still. (Its 'trembling lady' nickname reflects a tendency to vibrate when large numbers cross at once.)

Tolls were eliminated early on, but the two booths remain, and alongside the 4,000 bulbs that light it up at night give it a festive, seaside atmosphere.

Look out for the wartime notices at the entrances, warning troops to break step whilst crossing the bridge.

There was an ancient ford where **Chelsea Bridge** now spans the river. This one dates from the 1930s. The first bridge here was named after Queen Victoria, but when it was found to be structurally weak its moniker was swiftly changed to Chelsea in case it collapsed, dragging the royal family's name into the mud. The bridge's towers and cables are lit from below at night by light-emitting diodes.

The original **Vauxhall Bridge**, completed in 1816, was the first iron bridge over the Thames, but when the Metropolitan Board of Works bought it in 1879 (and, as usual, got rid of the tolls) they discovered that its central piers were already badly eroded.

The replacement bridge of 1906 was widely attacked for its stark ugliness, but a redeeming feature for those who like such things is the series of monumental bronze statues above the piers. They're not visible from the bridge itself, but from the shore you can see figures representing Agriculture, Architecture, Engineering and Pottery on the upstream piers and Science, Fine Arts, Local Government and Education from downstream.

And tunnels, too

The Thames Tunnel, running from Rotherhithe to Wapping, was the world's first underwater tunnel, masterminded from 1823 over a period of 18 years by Marc Brunel and his son Isambard.

Today there are more subterranean routes under the London river, tube lines and all, than any other in the world, but in those pioneering days the work was especially dangerous. The Cornish miners employed on the job were often struck down by an affliction known as tunnel sickness. Brunel senior's diary records dead and dying labourers and blames the 'excessively offensive' air, no doubt deriving from sewage-steeped earth: 'It affects the eyes. I feel much debility after having been some time below.'

Brunel junior, then 21, almost lost his life in January 1828 when the river burst through the roof and trapped him beneath a beam. Struggling free, he was washed to the shaft of the tunnel, where he banged on a locked door and was released. (It was while recuperating from this ordeal in the West Country that he heard about a competition to design the Clifton Suspension Bridge.)

The American novelist Nathaniel Hawthorne described the 365 m (1,200 ft) Thames Tunnel as 'an arched corridor that extends into everlasting midnight. Gloomily lighted with jets of gas at regular intervals – plastered at the sides, and stone beneath the feet. It would have made an admirable prison.'

Originally a foot tunnel, it had small shops running along it, but it was never popular. In 1870 it was taken over by the East London Railway Company – although it would be another 20 years before the first purpose-built tube tunnel was dug out between King William Street and Stockwell south of the river.

Afficionados of pedestrian tunnels can explore two close together in the borough of Greenwich: Greenwich tunnel (370 m; 1,215 ft) links the Cutty Sark to Island Gardens, Tower Hamlets, while the Woolwich tunnel (504 m; 1,654 ft) runs between Woolwich and North Woolwich, Newham.

The Friends of Greenwich and Woolwich foot tunnels (FOGWOFT) was set up in 2013, and both have been modernised, incorporating an Ethos Active Mobility system to monitor and manage tunnel usage.

Pairs of stone pinecones embellish the obelisks at either end of **Lambeth Bridge**, although urban myth prefers to believe that they're supposed to be pineapples in honour of the famous plant hunter John Tradescant the Younger – a local resident said to have first introduced the fruit to Britain in the 17th century. This is another replacement for a failed earlier structure, and it dates from 1932.

It's almost obligatory to quote Wordsworth's sonnet on **Westminster Bridge**, from where he observed that 'the river glideth at his own sweet will':

Earth has not anything to show more fair:
Dull would he be of soul who could pass by
A sight so touching in its majesty . . .

The poet wouldn't recognise either the majesty of today's Palace of Westminster at the bridge's end, because it was rebuilt after a disastrous fire some thirty years after he wrote those lines, or the bridge itself, which was replaced at about the same time. The architect Charles Barry was responsible for them both.

- The bridge was officially opened at 3.45 a.m. on 24 May, 1862 – the exact moment at which Queen Victoria had been born 43 years before.

- Westminster Bridge is painted green, which is the colour of the leather seats in the House of Commons, while the red of Lambeth Bridge (at the corresponding end of Parliament) matches the seats in the House of Lords.

- The imperious Coade stone lion at the end of the bridge looks to have been made for the site, but it stood on the parapet of the Lion Brewery a little downstream, and it has been there only since 1966.

- In March 2017 an Islamic terrorist drove a van into pedestrians on the bridge, killing four and injuring around fifty. He then fatally stabbed a police officer before being shot dead. (Concrete bollards have since been erected on several London bridges as a countermeasure.)

The **Hungerford Railway Bridge** and the flanking pedestrian **Golden Jubilee Bridges** run together across the river from the south to Charing Cross station. Isambard Brunel designed a suspension footbridge here in 1845.

Brunel's original brick pile buttresses remain today, but when a dedicated railway bridge replaced Brunel's footbridge some 20 years later the chains were re-used in the Clifton Suspension Bridge over a gorge in Bristol.

Footways ran alongside the new bridge. One of them was still in use in the 1990s, but it was in such a poor state a decision was taken to create a new deck on either side. The new bridges, supported by outward-leaning pylons, were opened in 2002, won a Royal Fine Art Commission building of the year award and (with 8.5 million footfalls a year) this is now the busiest pedestrian crossing on the Thames.

Waterloo Bridge, which has the South Bank area at its southern end (including the National Theatre and the London Eye), dates from the Second World War, though a predecessor opened in 1817 – and had an unfortunate reputation as a place for suicide attempts.

- In September 1978 the exhiled Bulgarian dissident Georgi Markov was poisoned by a ricin-filled pellet fired from an adapted umbrella while waiting for a bus on the bridge.

A bridge too far-fetched

The controversial Garden Bridge, a proposed pedestrian crossing between Waterloo and Blackfriars bridges complete with tree plantings, emptied £46 million from the public purse before the idea was thrown out.

First promoted by the actress Joanna Lumley, and supported by the then mayor of London, Boris Johnson, the bridge received planning permission in 2014 and would have opened from six in the morning until midnight each day – except for up to a dozen occasions a year when private functions would be held in order to pay for its maintenance.

Soon after taking over as mayor of London in May 2016, Sadiq Khan declared that no more money would be spent on the bridge, its cost by then having risen from the original estimate of £60 million to £185 million. As the figure continued to rise, two major donors pulled out, and in August 2017 the Garden Bridge Trust abandoned the project.

A BBC correspondent described the affair as 'an embarrassing mess for the capital', leading to fierce arguments about who was to blame for wasting so much public money.

Blackfriars Bridge is an 1869 replacement of a structure opened a century before and known as the William Pitt Bridge. The River Fleet, now underground, joins the Thames here.

- The ends of the bridge are shaped like a pulpit as a reference to the Black Friars of the Dominican priory which stood nearby.

- Those sturdy red pillars next to it are the supports of the old railway bridge pulled down in 1985.

- Note the sculptor John Birnie Philip's stone carvings of birds on the piers – those on the downstream side showing marine life and seabirds, those facing upstream depicting freshwater birds.

- In June 1982 the body of Roberto Calvi – known as 'God's banker' because of his close association with the Vatican – was found hanging from one of the arches. Five Mafia suspects were acquitted in a Rome court in 2007 for lack of evidence.

The **Millennium Footbridge** from Bankside to the City opened in 2000, but it shook so much (becoming known as the Wobbly Bridge) that it was closed for two years for modifications.

Known as the Iron Bridge, the original **Southwark Bridge** features in Dickens' novels – and in *Little Dorritt* the toll is given as a penny. The present crossing opened in 1921. Its limp claim to fame is that it has the lowest traffic use of all the central London bridges.

As we've seen, the Romans built the first **London Bridge** – and there have been several since. The medieval one, built between 1176 and 1209, sported houses, a chapel and a gatehouse, and its 19 arches became increasingly narrow over the years as new timbers were introduced to bolster the piers. Boats could only just pass beneath it at high tide, and at other times the rushing waters were perilous, watermen drowning as they shot the rapids.

'London Bridge', the saying went, 'was made for wise men to go over and fools to go under.'

The houses were cleared away during the 18th century, and the two central arches were replaced by a single span, but a new bridge was badly needed, and it eventually arrived in 1831.

By the end of the century the bridge was the busiest spot in London, and it was sinking at the rate of 2.5 cm (an inch) every eight years – and more to the east than the west. Yet another replacement was in the offing, and today's concrete box-girder bridge was duly opened by the Queen in 1973.

• The gatehouse of the medieval London Bridge was the scene of gruesome displays. The heads of executed notables would be preserved by dipping them in lard and boiling them before impaling them on spikes for all to see – a fate befalling, among many others, Jack Cade, Thomas More and Thomas Cromwell.

• In the 1960s the 1831 bridge was sold to an American businesman, who had it rebuilt at Lake Havasu City, Arizona – but an inland arch survives a few metres downstream of the present bridge.

• In June 2017 three Islamic terrorists used a rented van to mow down pedestrians on the bridge before driving to the nearby Borough Market and stabbing people at random. Eight of their victims died and 48 were injured before armed police shot the men dead.

East Acton

Notting Dale

Wormholt Farm

Shepherds Bush

Sir R.º South's Observatory

K...
Palace

Starch Green

Holland Ho.

Kens...

Brook Green

...on

...am Green

Hammersmith

W. LON
CEME

Walkams Green

Sneakenhall

Barnes Elms

Craven Cot.

Palace

Parsons Green

Barnes

Fulham

Barnes Common

Putney

...een

North Field

Wandsworth

Putney Park

South Field

Roehampton Gate

Roehampton

Bayswater

HYDE PARK

Kensington

Gardens

The River

Knightsbridge

Brompton

GREEN PARK

ST JAMES PARK

Palace

ngton

Old Brompton

Little Chelsea

Chelsea

Hospital

T H A M E S

H

Red Ho.

Nine Elms

DEPOT

St Lamb

Battersea Fields

RAILROAD

Battersea New Town

Battersea

Stockwell

SOUTHAMPTON

Clapham

LONDON

Station

Battersea Rise

Clapham Common

Wandsworth Common

The area from London Bridge down to Limehouse (just above Canary Wharf), is known as the Pool of London, and the river passes under one last bridge along the way – the daddy of them all, **Tower Bridge**.

When it was planned in the 1870s sailing ships still came up the river to the deep port facilities in the Upper Pool. Since a conventional bridge would have been too low – a design by Joseph Bazalgette was rejected for this reason – the preferred solution was the 'bascule' system, by which two central leaves rise to create a headroom of 41m (135 ft). Although the original hydraulic operating system was modernised in 1974, to outward appearances nothing has changed – and the bridge opens around a thousand times a year.

The bascules lie between two large towers built on piers, with suspension bridges over smaller spans on either side. While traffic and pedestrians cross 44 m (143 ft) above the river at high tide, there is also a higher level, open-air walkway – now part of a Tower Bridge Exhibition tour which includes the towers and the Victorian engine rooms.

The bascules are opened just enough to allow safe passage, except (a peculiarly British form of decorum) when members of the royal family are on board, when they are raised as far as they will go.

- There was a famous close call in December 1952 when the bridge began to be raised just as a No. 27 double-decker bus reached the southern bascule. The driver, Albert Gunter, having to make a split-second decision, accelerated over a 0.9 m (3 ft) gap and the bus dropped 1.8 m (6 ft) onto the north bascule. Gunter was given a small cash reward for his initiative by the City Corporation.

- In April 1968 Flt Lt Alan Pollock, aggrieved that there was to be no fly-past to mark the RAF's 50th birthday, flew his Hawker Hunter jet fighter past the House of Parliament and through the bridge. He was discharged from the RAF on medical grounds.

- In 1973 Paul Martin, a stockbroker's clerk on bail after charges of stock-market fraud, twice flew a single-engine Beagle Pup through the bridge, 'buzzed' buildings in the City – and then headed north for the Lake District, where he crashed his plane and was killed.

- In August 1999 Jef Smith, a 60-year-old Freeman of the City of London, exercised an ancient right by driving a 'flock' of (two) sheep over the bridge in order to highlight the erosion of pensioners' rights.

- In October 2003 a Fathers 4 Justice campaigner, David Crick, climbed a tower crane near Tower Bridge dressed as Spiderman. Police closed the bridge and surrounding roads, causing widespread traffic congestion across the City.

London abridged

**Thumbnail sketches of what to see as
you pass downriver under London's bridges**
L= left bank; R= right bank

Beyond Albert Bridge, the four chimneys of
Battersea Power Station (R) are unmissable.
Coal-fired, and built in stages from 1929, it
became the biggest brick building in Europe.
Designed by Sir Giles Gilbert Scott, it has lavish
Art Deco interiors and was declared a heritage
site after closing in 1975.

The far from bashful cream-and-green stepped
fortress at **Vauxhall Cross** (R) is the HQ of the
British secret-service arm MI6. It's on the site of
the former Vauxhall Gardens (p.150).

Formerly the Tate Gallery, **Tate Britain** (L) on
Millbank houses the nation's finest collection of
UK art. Its founder, Sir Henry Tate, made his
fortune from sugar cubes.

Lambeth Palace (R) has been the London seat
of the Archbishops of Canterbury since the
13th century. The chapel and the crypt beneath
it survive from that period, Morton's Tower
was built in 1490 and there have been many
refashionings through the ages.

Charles Barry's **Houses of Parliament** (L) cover 3.2 ha (8 acres) and incorporate a hundred staircases, more than a thousand rooms and 3.2 km (two miles) of passageways. The famous clock tower is commonly known as Big Ben, although the name actually refers specifically to the hour bell.

The misnamed **Cleopatra's Needle** on the Embankment (L) – it dates from a much earlier period than the famous queen – is a 18 m (60 ft) pink granite column carved with dedications to gods and pharaohs. Erected in the Egyptian city of Heliopolis in 1475BC, it was carried off to Alexandria by the Roman emperor Augustus some 1,500 years later. It eventually toppled over into the sand, and it was presented to Britain in 1819 by the Turkish viceroy of Egypt. You can see its twin in Central Park, New York.

The **South Bank** (R), between Westminster and Blackfriars bridges, is an arts and tourist area which includes the Royal Festival Hall and the National Theatre. The first striking feature you'll come across is the **London Eye**, billed as 'the tallest observation wheel in the western hemisphere'. For the record, a ride in one of the pods will take you up above London to a height of 135 m (443 ft).

The window glazing bars promoting a brand of beef stock cubes on the **Oxo Tower** (R) were a blatant device to get round a ban on illuminated signs after the Liebig Extract Meat Company bought this former power station in the 1920s and adapted it (in Art Deco fashion) for use as a cold store. Today there's a restaurant on the top floor.

The domed **St Paul's Cathedral** (L) was the noblest of many churches rebuilt by Sir Christopher Wren after the fire of 1666. It's been the scene of many funerals, weddings and thanksgiving services with a national significance.

After London Bridge look out for **The Shard** (R), the iconic skyscraper with great views from the top, and for the former **Billingsgate Market** (L), a handsome building the past of which is remembered in the large fish on the weather-vanes at either end.

The **Tower of London** (L) begun by William the Conqueror in 1078, holds the Crown Jewels, but in the public imagination it's a byword for medieval punishment. Prisoners brought here for execution through the **Traitors' Gate** include Sir Thomas More, Thomas Cromwell and two of Henry VIII's discarded wives.

After his work on the similar project at Battersea, Sir Giles Gilbert Scott was employed to improve the look of the Bankside Power Station – since decommissioned, and now better known as that gaunt cathedral to contemporary art, **Tate Modern** (R).

Thatched roofs went out of fashion after the fire of 1666, and the one atop **Shakespeare's Globe** (R) is said to be the first to appear in central London since then. The Globe opened in 1997, close to the site of the bard's theatre, and is an attempt to recreate the look and atmosphere of the Elizabethan original.

Southwark Cathedral (R) was formerly the church of an Augustinian priory, itself built on the site of a Roman villa – and part of a Roman pavement can be seen inside.

The Great Fire of London started in a baker's shop in Pudding Lane. **The Monument** (L) which commemorates it – a fluted Doric column – stands 62 m (202 ft) from that spot and is an exactly matching 62 m tall.

HMS *Belfast* (R), launched in 1938 and the largest cruiser ever built for the Royal Navy, is moored above Tower Bridge as a museum ship. Her exploits included a role in sinking the German battleship *Scharnhorst* in 1943.

‘ Behold the wonder of
this present age,
A famous river now
become a stage:
Question not what I now
declare to you.
The Thames is now both
fair and market too. ’

CHAPTER EIGHT

GOING UP THE RIVER

From medieval times until the Victorian age the Lord Mayor's Show was a vibrant Thames spectacle. The livery companies decked out barges in competitive array and a gaudy flotilla accompanied the new incumbent upriver from the City of London, where he held sway, to swear allegiance to the monarch at Westminster.

The pageant had its rowdy elements (in 1453 one of the revellers was killed in a skirmish between the Merchant Taylors and the Skinners), but that only made it a typical Thames occasion – organised merriment on the water, with a splash of anarchy thrown in.

Vauxhall Gardens

Several pleasure gardens were developed close to the Thames, their visitors soaking up the carefree riverine atmosphere – and the one at Vauxhall was the most famous of them all.

Samuel Pepys paid a visit in 1667, when it was still known by its original name of New Spring Garden – and when, before the building of Vauxhall Bridge, it could be reached from the northern bank of the river only by boat.

It was diverting, he wrote in his diary, 'to hear the nightingale and other birds, and here fiddles and there a harp, and here a Jew's trump and here laughing and there fine people walking'.

During the following century there were extravagant additions, including supper rooms, artificial ruins, water spectacles and several buildings in the Chinese style. The gardens were lit at night by lamps hanging in the trees; paying customers were entertained by musicians, tightrope walkers and balloonists; and there were , of course, handy alcoves for secret assignations. It closed in 1859.

Bazalgette's Embankment killed it, because the narrowing of the river made it difficult for oarsmen to row against what had become a much swifter tide. The Lord Mayor's Show* became a procession of 'floats' through the streets, as it is today – although in recent years a river pageant with fireworks has been reintroduced as a colourful accompaniment.

frost fairs

Flowing water wasn't necessary for Thames dwellers to have a good time. Before the era of bridge building the river was both wider, shallower and more sluggish. On numerous occasions over the centuries temperatures plummeted sufficiently for the water to freeze.

During the bleak winter of 1434–5, for example, the Thames was solid for well over two months, and people could walk on it from London Bridge almost as far as Gravesend.

* The Lord Mayor shouldn't be confused with the Mayor of London – a political, much more powerful figure. He or she represents the City of London and is the champion of its financial institutions.

In 1536 Henry VIII travelled by sleigh from Westminster to Greenwich, and in 1565 the chronicler Raphael Holinshed saw boys 'who played at football there as boldly as if it had been on dry land; diverse of the court shot daily at pricks [targets] set up on the Thames'.

Most fun of all, though, were the celebrated frost fairs that took advantage of the freeze-up several times between 1608 and 1814. A pamphlet in the British Museum records one held in a particularly chilly winter, when the ice was 45 cm (18 in) thick.

GREAT BRITAIN'S WONDER:

Being a true Representation of a prodigious Frost, which began about the beginning of December 1683, and continued till the fourth day of February following, and held on with such violence that men and beasts, coaches and carts, went as frequently thereon as boats were wont to pass before. There was also a street of booths built from the Temple to Southwark, where were sold all sorts of goods imaginable, namely cloaths, plate, earthenware, meat, drink brandy, tobacco and a hundred sorts of other commodities not here inserted: it being the wonder of this present age.

This last phrase was picked up in a quatrain of celebratory verse:

Behold the wonder of this present age,
A famous river now become a stage:
Question not what I now declare to you.
The Thames is now both fair and market too.

On the packed ice there were booths and shops, bull- and bear-baiting, carriage racing, and hustlers and hucksters of every kind. The diarist John Evelyn emphasised the moral looseness this glassy gala encouraged, noting 'puppet plays and interludes, cookes, tipling and other lewd places, so that it seemed a bacchanalian triumph or carnival on the water'.

Thousands thronged the river for the very last fair in 1814, when the star attraction – proving the stability of the ice – was a parading elephant. The event was, as ever, an opportunist's paradise.

'Several tradesmen, who at other times were deemed respectable', reads a report, 'attended with their wares, and sold books, toys and trinkets of almost every description.'

A frozen river, we should add, could be the ruination of fishermen and watermen put out of work, while the aftermath was often a swift thaw followed by treacherous flooding.

Pleasure on Thames

The licence to have a good time on the water was enshrined in law in 1885, when the Thames Preservation Act ruled that 'The Thames is a navigable highway and has come to be largely used as a place of public recreation and resort; and it is expedient that provision should be made that it should be preserved as a place of regulated public recreation.'

There was such a surge in the use of the river during this period that there had to be an element of supervision. Huge numbers of weekend trippers – on a fine summer's day more than 6,000 would take the train from London to Henley – came to mess about in boats, cast their lines for fish, picnic on the banks or eat and drink at a riverside inn.

This carefree, no-holds-barred day out was known as 'Going up the river'.

Sticky wickets

From ice fairs to riverbed cricket ...

The immediate effect of the demolition of the old London Bridge in the 1830s was to bring about a dramatic fall in water levels upstream. The tightly packed piers had held back the downstream flow, but now it rushed away and sat some 76 cm (30 in) lower at Teddington.

During a dry spell in June 1884 the *Richmond and Twickenham Times* observed that 'The Thames . . . seems to be rapidly approaching the condition of those tropical streams which disappear altogether in the summer months.'

Ten years later the problem would be solved by a new lock at Richmond. In the meantime the river was sometimes so dried up that it would take a bouncing ball.

'People have dined and played cricket matches on the bed of the stream', *The Globe* reported, 'and waggish persons have affixed notices with the legend "Land to be let for building purposes. Apply to the Thames Conservancy."'

We've already heard the *Three Men in a Boat* narrator complaining about steam-launches. Some of them, he tells us, rubbed salt in the wound by towing houseboats behind.

> There is a blatant bumptiousness about a steam-launch that has the knack of rousing every evil instinct in my nature . . . The expression of the man who, with his hands in his pockets, stands by the stern, smoking a cigar, is sufficient to excuse a breach of the peace by itself; and the lordly whistle for you to get out of the way would, I am confident, ensure a verdict of 'justifiable homicide' from any jury of river-men.

Noise and bustle had infiltrated the tranquility of the upper Thames, but in contrast with the brashness of this cockney incursion there arose a code of gentility for the fashion-conscious day tripper. Here's Jerome's narrator again, remembering an excursion with two 'ladies':

> They were both beautifully got up – all lace and silky stuff, and flowers and ribbons and dainty shoes and light gloves. But they were dressed for a photographic studio, not for a river picnic. They were the 'boating costumes' of a French fashion plate. It was ridiculous fooling about in them anywhere near real earth, air and water.

Perhaps they'd been reading the *Thames Tide and Fashionable River Gazette*, which gave advice not only on what to wear on board (straw hats for men, with striped flannel coats over white shirts and trousers; navy or black serge dresses for women, with long suede gloves and elaborate hats as accessories), but how to deck out their houseboats with flowers to make them surrogate Hanging Gardens of Babylon.

fishermen's foe

The late 19th century was the heyday of angling clubs on the Thames, which attracted some 30,000 Londoners as members. A competitive breed, they had a murderous contempt for the otter.

'The animal is generally alluded to in more vituperative language than would have been thought to exist in the vocabulary of the "gentle" angler', reads a contemporary account, 'and should the death of the poor beast be compassed, the glory supposed to attach to the exploit is ludicrously out of proportion to the occasion.'

With a reward offered for their skins, otters were hunted practically to extinction.

A prized coat and badge

Rowing on the Thames was originally a practical or commercial activity, but it has long been a sport, too, and the oldest annual race on the river – indeed, in the world – dates back more than 300 years.

The Doggett's Coat and Badge (a name shared by the race itself and the prize awarded to the winner) was at first rowed between two pubs – the Swan at London Bridge and the Swan at Chelsea. Today's route is similar, passing under eleven bridges on the 7.4 km (4.6 miles) between London Bridge and Cadogan Pier.

Its founder was the Irish actor and comedian Thomas Doggett who, when joint manager of the Drury Lane Theatre early in the 18th century, was a regular user of the river 'taxis' and was clearly grateful for the service he received. In 1715 he offered a prize to the fastest of six young watermen in their first year of 'freedom' – that is, having come through their apprenticeships – and he left money in his will to keep the race going for ever. It shows every sign of doing so.

In the early years competitors used their working wherries, and would take almost two hours hauling against an outgoing tide. These days the young watermen use modern single sculling boats on an incoming tide and expect to complete the course in about half an hour.

First prize is a traditional watermen's red coat, adorned by a silver badge bearing the word 'Freedom' and the House of Hanover's heraldic horse: Doggett was a fervent Whig in politics and wished to celebrate the accession of George I to the throne. Each competitor gets a Doggett's lapel badge, and the Fishmongers' Company throws in cash prizes for the rowing clubs of the first four men home.

The toffs' race

Well within living memory the Oxford and Cambridge Boat Race was a fixture in the calendar which even people who'd never been within sight of a university campus got excited about. Its glamour has faded somewhat in a world with so many competing events, but it still attracts crowds of around 250,000 along the banks between Putney and Mortlake.

This snaking 'Championship Course' measures 6.8 km (4.2 miles), with the north station ('Middlesex') having the advantage of the first and last bends, and the south ('Surrey') station the longer middle bend. Small University Boat Race stones on the southern bank mark the starting and finishing points.

The clubs' presidents toss to choose their position on the water, after which the coxes attempt to maneouvre their boats to take advantage of the faster current in the middle of the river. This often brings a vigorous clashing of blades, with warnings from the umpire.

The race is rowed upstream and timed to start on an incoming flood tide so that the crews row with the fastest possible current, but things can get decidedly choppy if the wind blows in the 'wrong' direction, from the south-west.

• Boats have sunk on several occasions – and both of them during foul weather in 1912.

• There has been just one dead heat, in 1877 – those disputing the verdict unkindly pointing out that the race judge was over 70 and blind in one eye.

- In 1987 the US rower Chris Clark, smarting at Cambridge's victory the previous year, recruited four American post-graduates to boost the Oxford squad. Unfortunately they fell out with their coach, Dan Topolski, and shortly before the race they were dropped in favour of the university's reserve crew, Isis. Oxford, although underdogs, won by four lengths.

Head of the River

The remarkable Head of the River Race is held every March on the University Boat Race course, but from Mortlake to Putney and on an ebb tide.

It couldn't be more different. For one thing it's 'processional', which means the men's eights involved set off at ten-second intervals and are racing against the clock. It's also far busier: not just the two crews, but more than 400 of them.

A more modest affair when founded by the rowing coach Steve Fairbairn in 1925, the race now attracts competitors from around the world – predominantly from Europe, but also from as far afield as China, Australia and the USA.

- In 2012 the race was stopped for half an hour when a political protester, the Australian Trenton Oldfield, swam between the boats near Chiswick Pier. He was later fined and sentenced to six months' imprisonment.

Henley Regatta

When the first university boat race was organised in 1829 by two childhood friends – one a student at Christ Church, Oxford, the other at St John's College, Cambridge – they chose to stage it on the longest naturally straight stretch of the winding Thames they could find. This was 1.6 km (1 mile) long, and it wasn't in London, but at Henley.

This proved significant. Although the Oxford v Cambridge event switched to the capital, other races began to be held at Henley and were soon attracting large crowds. The town responded by organising a 'grand challenge cup' for men's eights, and in 1839 Henley Regatta was born. 'Its peculiar attractions', said one of its champions, Captain Edmund Gardiner, would be 'a source of amusement and gratification to the neighbourhood and the public in general.'

The Marchioness disaster

There's something particularly shocking about death striking unawares during moments of innocent happiness, and so it was with the sinking of the *Marchioness* in the early hours of 20 August, 1989.

The pleasure steamer, which had been one of the 'little boats' at Dunkirk in the Second World War, had been hired for a birthday party and was close to Cannon Street railway bridge when she was struck by the dredger *Bowbelle*.

Pierced by the dredger's anchor, the *Marchioness* rolled over, her superstructure became completely detached and she sank within 30 seconds. 51 people drowned.

A report blamed poor look-outs on the two vessels, both of which had been using the centre of the river. The government called for the creation of a new search and rescue service for the tidal Thames, as a result of which the Royal National Lifeboat Institution set up four lifeboat stations at Gravesend, Tower, Chiswick and Teddington.

flashing blades

It's impossible to exaggerate the sheer intensity of rowing on the Thames.

- There are more than 40 major rowing clubs along the non-tidal river and the Tideway, plus many smaller ones and around 20 university and 40 school clubs.

- The Henley event is among some 40 regattas held every year for men, women and junior rowers.

- There are more than 40 head of the river and long-distances races, most of them held on the Championship Course in London.

- Lakes adjacent to the Thames and dedicated to competitive rowing include Dorney Lake in Buckinghamshire, the Redgrave Pinsent Rowing Lake in Oxfordshire and Royal Albert Dock.

Rowing is of course its main business – 'A rowing life is not complete if it does not include competing at Henley', the organisers like to boast – but for many visitors it's simply an excuse for a five-day jamboree. The Regatta had Royal stuck in front of its name after Prince Albert paid a visit in 1851, and it quickly became a highlight of the social season.

- Since Prince Albert paved the way, every reigning monarch has maintained the tone by agreeing to be its patron.

- The Leander Club, founded in 1818 and based at Remenham along the river from Henley, claims to be the world's oldest rowing club – and its members have won more Olympic and World Championship medals than any other club in the world.

- The Regatta costs £2 million to stage each year.

- Racegoers get through 4,500 bottles of champagne and about a tonne of strawberries.

The Stewards' Enclosure, on the Berkshire side of the river, lies close to the finish line and comprises grandstands, a restaurant marquee and bars.

This is the place to be for the fashionable set. It has a waiting list of several years, and you aren't allowed in unless you obey a strict dress code: women must wear skirts or dresses that cover the knee and they're 'encouraged to wear a hat', while for men it's 'a lounge suit, blazer and flannels or evening dress and a tie'.

Ah, those blazers! Here's an outsider's view from the US rowing champion Jack Carlson, a past Regatta winner and the author of a book devoted to the subject:

The rowing blazer is designed to impress, intimidate and influence in a game of one-upmanship. But it's not about anything so mundane as socio-economic class; it's about letting other rowers and cognoscenti know what one has achieved in the sport and where one's loyalties lie.

Like the court liveries and heraldic devices of medieval Europe, the street gang colors of Compton and the patches and badges of Boy Scouts and Hell's Angels, rowing blazers are tribal totems, ceremonial vestments worn to emphasise both difference and belonging within their own little world.

The Thames itself can feel like its own little world for those who go up the river to escape the cares of life. Let's return to Mole in *The Wind in the Willows*, captivated by his first experience of the river.

'Do you know,' he said, 'I've never been in a boat before in all my life.'

'What?' cried the Rat, open-mouthed. 'Never been in a – you never – well, I – what have you been doing then?'

'Is it so nice as all that?' asked Mole shyly.

'Nice? It's the only thing,' said the Water Rat solemnly. 'Believe me, my friend, there is nothing half so much worth doing as messing about in boats.'

Tarka comes home

In 1957 the Natural History Museum declared the polluted Thames to be biologically dead, and two years later the *Manchester Guardian* – echoing newspapers from the Victorian era – claimed that the tidal reaches were 'a badly managed sewer', reporting that 'no oxygen is to be found in it for several miles above and below London Bridge'.

Today, thanks to changing industrial practices and government regulations, the Thames is widely regarded as the cleanest metropolitan river in the world. Non-biodegradable plastic is taking over from sewage as a growing menace, but the wildlife has come back.

• There are now 125 species of fish in the river , including the occasional salmon – and eels and lampreys have returned, too.

• A Zoological Society of London survey of the decade to 2014 reported 2,000 sightings of seals in the Thames, as well as hundreds of porpoises and dolphins – and even a bottlenose whale, which died after being stranded at Battersea.

169

- 400 species of invertebrates live in the river's mud, water and banks.

- Moorhens, herons and cormorants are among the waterfowl, waders and sea birds regularly to be seen in central London.

- The built-up environment makes it difficult for otters to colonise the urban Thames via its tributaries, but they're already sufficiently established upstream for anglers once again to be demanding that they be culled.

Naturalists visiting the upper reaches of the river should pencil in a visit to the Cotswold Water Park, a 10,400-hectare (40-square-mile) part of the Thames catchment area formerly given over to sand and gravel extraction. It's now an impressive lake system (147 of them in all), and an important refuge for a wide range of wildlife, and especially for wintering and breeding birds.

The Cotswold Water Park Trust manages six reserves open to the public, the Gloucester Wildlife Trust four and the Wiltshire Wildlife Trust another three. The Thames Path snakes through the lakes – and for those not interested in the wildlife there are areas for cycling, sailing and fishing, too.

At Cricklade, set amid this watery landscape, is North Meadow, one of Britain's few surviving unspoiled hay meadows. The time to visit is the spring, when its glory, the snake's head fritillary, is found in unrivalled numbers.

Downriver in the Barnes area is the **London Wetland Centre**, a reserve managed by the Wildfowl and Wetlands Trust and comprising four derelict Victorian reservoirs tucked into an arm of the Thames.

Spread over 100 ha (40 acres), it's home to many birds you won't find anywhere else in London – 'nationally significant' numbers of gadwall and northern shoveler, plus species such as Eurasian bittern, northern pintail, northern lapwing, water rail, Eurasian sparrowhawk, sand martin, common kingfisher, little grebe and great crested grebe.

Another resident is the rose-ringed parakeet, although that's hardly surprising: these raucous, striking bright-green immigrants (the earliest ones are presumed to have escaped from aviaries) can congregate in flocks up to 6,000 strong, and they've become a common presence in the gardens of Kingston and Twickenham.

❝A haze rested on the low shores that ran out to sea in vanishing flatness. The air was dark above Gravesend, and farther back still seemed condensed into a mournful gloom, brooding motionless over the biggest, and the greatest, town on earth.❞

CHAPTER NINE

DOWN TO THE SEA

Beyond Tower Bridge the sea calls, although we're still 14.5 km (9 miles) from the Thames Barrier and some 65 km (40 miles) from the estuary. In his novel *Millennium People*, J. G. Ballard places the change in atmosphere even further upriver:

The Thames shouldered its way past Blackfriars Bridge, impatient with the ancient piers, no longer the passive stream that slid past Chelsea Marina, but a rush of ugly water that had scented the open sea and was ready to make a run for it.

That restless current would once have barged its way past the wharves and cranes of noisome working docks – but no longer.

The old docks area has been cleaned up, handed over to finance, gentrified.* We pass Wapping (where the Prospect of Whitby claims to be London's oldest riverside pub), then up-and-coming Bermondsey, Rotherhithe and Limehouse, before arriving at the Isle of Dogs and (where vast amounts of sugar were once unloaded at the West India Docks) the gleaming glass towers of Canary Wharf.

This 'urban enterprise zone' has sprung up within the space of 30 years. The towering One Canada Square, completed in 1991, was then the tallest building in Europe, and it held that record for the UK until the Shard outdid it some 20 years later.

Although the area is part glossily residential and part entertainments hub – restaurants, cafes, shopping malls, cinemas, summer concerts, winter skating rink – it's above all a financial centre, now rivalling the City of London to the west.

---

* And yet hundreds of ships still pass through the docks every year – some commercial boats, plus luxury yachts, cruise liners and navy vessels.

More than 100,000 people work here, the office space measures around 1.5 million km^2 (16 million square feet) and it's the headquarters for finance houses from around the world.

These vast changes have unsettled many. It's hardly believable that as recently as 1997 some Isle of Dogs residents launched a legal case against the developers because the new high-rise buildings interfered with their television signals. (Of course they lost.)

The writer Iain Sinclair has become an abrasive chronicler of the transformation of the east London he once knew.

When I think I'm moving across a city of memories, where I have lived and worked for fifty years, I find that, very soon, I lose the markers by which I have navigated, the beacons by which I know myself . . . I step out of my knowledge, to the tottering edge of an abyss known as 'the future' or 'the human contract'.

There's much more to come: the 70-km (43-mile) stretch from Tower Hamlets to the Isle of Sheppey and Southend in the estuary – grandly designated the Thames Gateway – has been earmarked for similar treatment.

Whose river is it?

The Thames belongs to everyone, but how easy is it to take a stroll beside the river as it runs through our capital city?

In 2013 *Lonely Planet* described the Thames Path here as 'among the finest urban walks on Earth', although a London Assembly report had already warned that the riverside was changing into a thin strip of affluence that it described as a 'sterile monoculture'.

More serious has been a steady encroachment by private companies and landowners to deny public access. The issue has become part of a wider debate about 'pseudo-public spaces' both by the river and elsewhere in London – open-air areas which appear free to use but which are owned by corporations.

A *Guardian* investigation in 2015 found that in places the Thames Path bore 'more resemblance to a high-security prison corridor than a public right of way: gates, spikes and CCTV warning notices stand sentinel over fragmented patches of riverside that start and end abruptly, and whose access rights are shrouded in a veil of bureaucratic obscurity'.

'The idea that London's spaces have always been open and democratic is a myth', the specialist writer Anna Minton said. 'It took a long, hard fight to bring streets under public control, and there is a constant push-back against it – if people aren't galvanised and engaged with these spaces then they will slip away into private hands.'

• Access to some of the best viewing areas for the Queen's diamond jubilee river pageant in 2012, including a number of streets on the south bank of the Thames, was restricted to wristband-wearing guests.

• Campaigners for better wages at Canary Wharf in 2012 were told by security guards that they were on private property and were shepherded onto a small strip of land outside the Jubilee line tube station. 'That's public land,' a spokesman said, 'and whenever there's a demonstration about anything on Canary Wharf they're directed to that little plot.'

• In 2017 the Labour leader, Jeremy Corbyn, called for Britain's pseudo-public spaces to be reclaimed from corporate interests, while the mayor of London, Sadiq Khan, promised to publish new guidelines on how public places were governed.

World class

Greenwich once throbbed with commercial life, with Henry VIII's naval dockyard at Deptford next door, but it also had a great royal palace where three monarchs were born. Today 'Maritime Greenwich' has been declared a World Heritage Site by UNESCO, describing its buildings as 'the finest and most dramatically sited architectural and landscape ensemble in the British Isles'.

Glorious though it is, the site has a chequered history. In 1616 James I had a new house begun here for his wife, Anne of Denmark – a gift, so the story goes, to apologise for swearing in front of her when she accidentally killed one of his favourite hounds during a hunt.

The **Queen's House** was no ordinary second home but the first Palladian building in Britain, designed by the classical architect Inigo Jones and standing just to the south of the medieval Palace of Placentia. By the time it was completed, around 1636, both the king and queen had died, and Charles I had given it in turn to his wife, Henrietta Maria.

Bad times were soon to follow, both for the king and the palace: the building was badly damaged in the civil war which led to his execution in 1649, and Charles II, after the Restoration, began to rebuild it but ran out of funds.

So matters stood until William and Mary came to the throne in the so-called Glorious Revolution of 1688. Mary decided that the partially restored palace should become a seamen's hospital, but she was insistent that the view of the Queen's House from the river shouldn't be obstructed. With that instruction in mind, Christopher Wren and his assistant Nicholas Hawksmoor designed separate buildings, with Inigo Jones's elegant house as their centrepiece.

This is the stunning complex we now know as the **Old Royal Naval College**, because that's what it became after the hospital closed in 1869. (Today it's part of the University of Greenwich.) Its greatest attractions inside are the neo-classical chapel and the ceiling of the painted hall which it took the artist Sir James Thornhill 20 years to complete.

The **Royal Observatory**, which overlooks Greenwich from the Park, was also designed by Wren. The time ball introduced to the top of it in 1833 was the first visual time signal in the world – and to this day it's raised at 12.55 and dropped at precisely 13.00 so that ships on the Thames can set their clocks accurately.

It was at a conference in Washington in 1884 that Greenwich was declared the location of the Prime Meridian, or 0 degrees of longitude.

In **Flamsteed House**, which was Wren's original observatory building, you'll find London's only camera obscura.

The **Cutty Sark**, originally built in 1869, has had more dangerous moments in recent years than when she sailed the sea. She suffered a serious fire in 2007 while being restored, and another, smaller one seven years later.

A sleek black and gold British clipper, she at first carried tea before switching to the wool trade with Australia. She's part of the National Historic Fleet, the equivalent of a Grade I listed building.

Big tent

The Millennium Dome, designed by Richard Rogers, was controversial when it was built. The Labour prime minister, Tony Blair, claimed it would be 'a triumph of confidence over cynicism, boldness over blandness, excellence over mediocrity', while the Conservatives branded it 'banal, anonymous and rootless'. Today it houses the 02 Arena and has, after Manchester, the second-highest seating capacity of any indoor UK venue.

Up in the air

The cable car running across the Thames from the Greenwich Peninsula to the Royal Victoria Dock was another controversial project when it opened in 2012.

It was sponsored by the United Arab Emirates and the contract unusually forbids the mayor or Transport for London from ever criticising the UAE royal families, its government or the contract itself.

The Emirates Air Line crosses the water at a height of 90 m (300 ft), and the trip lasts ten minutes – five in the rush hour.

Salt in the nostrils

From Greenwich it's down to the Thames Barrier and beyond. These lower reaches of the river, wilder and less hospitable, often appear in literature as menacing and unsettling. Here's Joseph Conrad's narrator coming up the river in *Heart of Darkness*:

> *A haze rested on the low shores that ran out to sea in vanishing flatness. The air was dark above Gravesend, and farther back still seemed condensed into a mournful gloom, brooding motionless over the biggest, and the greatest, town on earth.*

Charles Dickens' Pip in *Great Expectations* visits his bleak local churchyard and realises that:

> *. . . the dark flat wilderness beyond the churchyard, intersected with dykes and mounds and gates, with scattered cattle feeding on it, was the marshes; and that the low leaden line beyond was the river; and that the distant savage lair from which the wind was rushing was the sea . . .*

Daniel Defoe, in his *Tour Through the Whole Island of Great Britain* (1727), had a chilling view of life in the Dengie marshes of Essex where the 'ague' took people off in droves.

Local men, he wrote, sometimes had up to fourteen or fifteen wives:

> . . . the reason being that they, being bred in the marshes themselves and seasoned to the place, did pretty well with it; but they always went into the hilly country ... for a wife, and when they took the young lasses into the marshes, they presently changed their complexion, got an ague or two, and seldom held it* above half a year, or a year at most.

No doubt this was an exaggeration, and no doubt the expanding, civilising influence of the Thames Gateway will one day dispel a dread of the sinister river. But it's still a doughty walker who goes the full length of the Thames Path to touch the tall London Stone at Yantlet Creek on the Isle of Grain – the mark of the City of London's jurisdiction 54 km (33.5 miles) as the crow flies from London Bridge.

One river, but many moods, and many varied tales to tell . . .

*That is, held onto life.

Glossary

Bascule bridge A bridge with a span that swings upwards to allow boats to pass through.

Brexit The UK's departure from the European Union.

Bummaree A middleman trader in the old Billingsgate market.

Cornelian A brownish-red mineral used as a semi-precious gemstone.

Costermonger A street seller.

Danelaw The northern part of Britain ceded to Viking invaders.

Eyot A small island in the Thames.

Fatberg A large mass of fat and other waste that builds up in the sewers.

Hulk Prison ships, as once in the Thames.

Hydropathy A water cure, regarded as an alternative medicine.

Legger A man employed to propel canal boats through tunnels with his feet.

Lighterman A waterman operating a small, flat-bottomed barge.

Livery company A City of London trade guild.

Tutelary god A deity or spirit protecting a particular place or group of people.

Wherry A small rowing boat used to ferry passengers across the Thames.

Whig A member of the political party that contested power with the Tories from the 1680s to the 1850s.

Thames timeline

54 BC First mention of the Thames in literature – by Julius Caesar after his second incursion into Britain.
AD 43 Roman invasion of Britain by Augustus is soon followed by building of the first London bridge.
634 King Cynegius is baptised in the Thames at Dorchester by Bishop Birinius.
838 Egbert holds Great Council at Kingston.
890 King Alfred holds first recorded English parliament, at Shifford.
1078 The Tower of London begun by William the Conqueror.
1197 Richard the Lionheart sells river rights to the Corporation of London.
1209 A second London Bridge replaces the Roman original.
1215 *Magna Carta* signed by King John at Runnymead.
1272 Edward I grants charter to the Worshipful Company of Fishmongers.
1285 London Stone raised near Staines Bridge to mark western extent of Corporation of London's jurisdiction.
1420s London's mayor, Dick Whittington, introduces 'longhouse' segregated lavatory at Cheapside.
1434–5 The Thames is solid ice for two months.
1514 Trinity House founded.
1515 Cardinal Wolsey builds Hampton Court Palace on the banks of the Thames.
1535 Act of Parliament attempts to protect the Thames from 'dung and filth'.
1616 The Queen's House at Greenwich begun by James I.
1620 The *Mayflower* leaves Rotherhithe on its journey taking the Pilgrim Fathers from Plymouth to America.

1647 The Putney Debates discuss the future of the constitution after the English Civil War.

1658 A bowhead whale runs aground at Greenwich.

1666 The Great Fire of London, after which much of the cityscape by the Thames is refashioned.

1667 Dutch warships come up the Thames to bombard Chatham.

1676 Christopher Wren's Royal Observatory opens at Greenwich.

1683–4 A severe winter is celebrated in one of the Thames 'frost fairs'.

1696 Work starts on Wren's Greenwich Hospital, now the Old Royal Naval College.

1701 Corporation of Watermen bans foul language by its members on the river.

1715 First Doggett's Coat and Badge race.

1717 Handel's *Water Music* is given its first performance as George I enjoys a pageant on the Thames.

1726 Putney Bridge becomes the first Thames bridge built in the capital since London Bridge.

1774 Henley Bridge swept away by floods.

1776 Hulks first moored in the Thames (until 1857).

1790 Opening of the West India Docks.

1795 Feminist author Mary Wollstonecraft attempts suicide by throwing herself off Putney Bridge.

1812 Opening of Teddington Lock as the new upper limit of the tidal Thames.

1814 The very last frost fair on the Thames.

1818 Leander Club, the world's oldest rowing club, founded at Remenham.

1828 Opening of St Katharine's Docks; Isambard Kingdom Brunel is badly injured while excavating the Thames Tunnel from Rotherhithe to Wapping.

1829 First Oxford versus Cambridge boat race – at Henley.

1830 Last hangings at Execution Dock, Wapping.
1832 A third London Bridge is built, replacing
the second.
1834 First of four major cholera outbreaks in London
(the others in 1849, 1854 and 1865); fire devastates the
Houses of Parliament.
1839 First Henley Regatta.
1855 Michael Faraday tests the contamination of the
Thames; opening of the Royal Victoria Dock.
1856 Joseph Bazalgette is appointed chief engineer of
the Metropolitan Board of Works (MBW).
1858 'The Great Stink.'
1862 Boating trip along the Thames near Oxford
during which Lewis Carroll begins *Alice in Wonderland*,
published three years later.
1868 Opening of Millwall Dock.
1870 Bazalgette's Victoria Embankment completed,
incorporating his new sewer system.
1877 MBW given permission to buy (and modernise)
all London bridges from Hammersmith to Waterloo.
1878 *Princess Alice* pleasure-boat disaster near
Woolwich Pier claims more than 600 lives; Cleopatra's
Needle erected on the Embankment.
1880 Royal Albert Dock opens at Gallion's Reach.
1885 The Thames Preservation Act enshrines the use
of the river for public recreation.
1886 Opening of Tilbury Docks.
1889 The Great Dock strike; publication of *Three Men
in a Boat*.
1894 Opening of Tower Bridge.
1908 Publication of *The Wind in the Willows*.
1909 Port of London Authority (PLA) founded;
boundary stone at Teddington marks division of
responsibilities between the Environment Agency
(upstream) and the PLA.

1912 King George V Dock at North Woolwich is the last of the London docks to open.

1927 Unveiling of Stanley Spencer's *The Resurrection, Cookham*.

1929 Battersea Power Station under construction.

1952 A double-decker bus leaps the gap after Tower Bridge begins to open in error.

1953 Canvey Island is engulfed during a severe storm, with 85 people killed.

1973 A fourth London bridge opens. The third is sold to an American entrepreneur.

1978 The Bulgarian dissident Georgi Markov is killed by a poison pellet fired into his leg on Waterloo Bridge.

1982 Thames Barrier opens; the body of 'God's banker', Roberto Calvi, is found hanging from Blackfriars Bridge.

1989 *Marchioness* pleasure steamer disaster.

2000 Tate Modern gallery opens in the former Bankside Power Station; the London Eye opens on the South Bank; Millennium Bridge opens and then closes for two years for corrections to its 'wobble'; Millennium Dome opens at Greenwich.

2012 Licences withrawn from Billingsgate porters, ending centuries-old tradition; cable car opens across the river from Greenwich to Royal Victoria Dock.

2014 Planning permission granted for a Garden Bridge over the Thames between Waterloo and Blackfriars – but two years later financial support is withdrawn.

2016 Work begins on the Tideway Tunnel, the first major sewer building since Bazalgette; Brexiteers and Remainers stage a water fight on the Thames at Westminster.

2017 Terrorist attacks on Westminster Bridge and London Bridge; a monstrous 'fatberg' is found in the sewers beneath Whitechapel.

Index